Around the year 2

by Brigitte Schanz-Hering

edited by Gillian Bathmaker-Vollmer

Ernst Klett Verlag
Stuttgart München Düsseldorf Leipzig

CONTENTS

Introduction 4

| | Teacher's notes page | Copy master page |

1 Going Back to School 5
    Two games for the first day of school 5
    About Labor Day in the USA 6
♪ ▭ Song: Wonderful World 6
    1.1 School is cool! 6 47
☆ 1.2 Two poems for the first day of school 7 48
    1.3 The great school race 7 49
☆ ▭ 1.4 Staying home from school 7 50

2 Autumn has come 8
    2.1 Autumn poems 8 51
✱ 2.2 Apple Harvest 8 52
    Chain game: I went to the greengrocer's 9
♪ ▭ Song: Raindrops keep fallin' on my head 9
    2.3 Weather wordsearch 10 53
    2.4 "That's the way the wind blows!" 11 54
    ✱ Wind and wind belts 11 54

3 Festivals in October and November 12
♪ ▭ Song: We are the World 12
    ☆ ✱ Africa's problems – our problems 13
    ✱ About United Nations Day and United Nations Universal Children's Day .. 13
✱ 3.1 Columbus Day and the discovery of America 13 55
    3.2 It's Hallowe'en 14 56
    ▭ About Hallowe'en 14
    Activities for Hallowe'en 15
✱ 3.3 Guy Fawkes' Night – 5th November 16 57
✱ ▭ About Guy Fawkes' Night 16
✱ 3.4 Thanksgiving – Fourth Thursday in November (USA) ... 16 58

4 Christmas is coming 17
♪ ▭ Song: Another Rock and Roll Christmas 17
    4.1 Christmas: Facts, fun and faith 18 59
    Christmas Quiz 18
    4.2 The Giant Christmas Crossword 19 60
    4.3 Christmas jokes 19 61
✱ 4.4 Christmas crackers 20 62
♪ ▭ Song: Last Christmas 20
    Further activities 21

5 New Year and Winter 22
    5.1 Nick's thank you letter 22 63
    Further activity for New Year 22
    About Hogmanay – New Year in Scotland 22
☆ 5.2 Happy "Chinese" New Year! 22 64
    ☆ About Chinese New Year 22
♪ ▭ Song: Winter Wonderland 23
✱ 5.3 Snow 24 65
☆ ✱ 5.4 Martin Luther King Day 24 66
☆ ✱ ▭ About Martin Luther King 24
♪ ▭ Song: Black, brown and white 25

6 Festivals in February and March 26
♪ 🖭 Song: When I'm sixty-four 26
    6.1 14th February – Valentine's Day 27 67
        🖭 About Valentine's Day 28
        Further activities 28
✶ 6.2 President's Day .... 29 .... 68/69
    6.3 Pancake Day 29 70
        🖭 About Pancake Day 29
♪ 🖭 6.4 Song: Paddy's Green Shamrock Shore 30 71
        About St Patrick's Day 30

7 Spring 30
☆ 🖭 7.1 The long winter 30 72
♪ 🖭 Song: Here comes the sun 31
    7.2 Snowman 32 73
✶ 7.3 The first day of spring 32 74
♪ 🖭 Song: Garden Song 32
✶ 7.4 Gardens, gardening and land use 33 75
    Further activities 33

8 Festivals in April and May 34
    8.1 Easter 34 76
🖭 8.2 Egg trouble again .... 34 .... 77/78
    Further activity 34
    8.3 April Fools' Day 35 79
    About April Fools' Day 35
    8.4 Mother's Day 35 80

9 Summer 36
♪ 🖭 Song: Summer in the city 36
☆ ✶ 9.1 A change in the Earth's climate 37 81
    9.2 London Trip 38 82
    Map of London 83
    Further activity 38
    🖭 Typically British: The Trooping of the Colour and the Wimbledon
    Lawn Tennis Championships 39
    Further activity 40
✶ 🖭 9.3 All American: Fourth of July and Flag Day 40 84
    ✶ Further activity 41
    9.4 American English (AE) – British English (BE) 41 85

10 School's out! 41
♪ 🖭 Song: Summer holiday 42
    10.1 Last day – at last! 43 86
    About school reports in Britain 44
✶ 10.2 European countries and their capitals 44 87
    Further activities 44
✶ 10.3 The Round Europe Race .... 44 .... 88/89
♪ 🖭 Song: Ice in the sunshine 45
    Games for the end of term 46

Items marked ✶ are suitable for use in cross-curricular or bi-lingual teaching.
Items marked ☆ are suitable for more advanced classes.
Items marked 🖭 and ♪ 🖭 are on the cassette which accompanies this book, Klett order number: 512744.

INTRODUCTION

Around the year 2 has been produced for pupils learning English in years 8, 9 and 10 in secondary schools (aged 13+). As the follow-up to *Around the Year* (Klett order number: 512741) it has been devised to supplement standard course books by providing a selection of lively and diverse material. There are songs, informative texts, puzzles, games, short stories, poems, listening comprehension exercises, and other activities all connected with festivals and events which take place throughout the year in Britain and America.

Around the year 2 is divided into two sections: teacher's notes and copy masters (worksheets). Both sections are divided into chapters, which are set in chronological order starting at the beginning and finishing at the end of the school year. Each chapter relates to a specific time of year or event in the year. The activities, worksheets, etc. within each chapter are arranged in a basic chronological and/or thematic order, although this order is by no means compulsory.

The teacher's notes are in the first section of the book and provide detailed suggestions for using the copy masters with solutions where applicable, as well as further background information, and ideas for games and further activities. The music, texts and activities that go with the songs are also included in the teacher's notes.

The copy masters in the second section of the book are intended to be copied and handed out to pupils. Pupils should be encouraged to keep all their handouts in a special folder, so that they gradually build up a complete "Around the year album". (Some pupils may already have an "Around the year album" with worksheets from the first volume of *Around the Year* in it. They can add the worksheets from *Around the Year 2* to this album.) The copy masters and activities can be used independently of each other, so teachers can make individual choices depending on the needs and demands of their classes and the time available. A number of the worksheets and activities are well-suited to cross-curricular or bi-lingual teaching. These are indicated ✲ on the contents page and in the teacher's notes. Worksheets which are suitable for more advanced classes are indicated ☆ on the contents page and in the teacher's notes.

Inevitably some of the vocabulary used will be new to pupils. Dictionaries should be available in the classroom for quick reference and teachers are well-advised to introduce important new vocabulary (either via the overhead projector or blackboard) before working with a worksheet.

The songs, sung by well-known pop artists, are all recorded on side 1 of the cassette (Klett order number: 512744). They are indicated ♪♪ ▭ on the contents page and in the teacher's notes. A number of the texts and the short stories are recorded on side 2 of the cassette. These are indicated ▭ on the contents page and in the teacher's notes.

The individual character of the worksheets and activities means that the teacher can use the material in *Around the year 2* regularly or sporadically (when time allows). The clear instructions in the teacher's notes mean that the material can also be used effectively when covering lessons for other teachers, even at short notice. Whatever the case, *Around the year 2* aims to liven up the classroom, motivate pupils and provide both pupils and teachers with a valuable insight into British and American culture and traditions.

TEACHER'S NOTES

1 Going back to school

Use the material in this chapter at the beginning of a new school year or a new term. Much of the material can also be used when school is being dealt with as a topic.

Two games for the first day of school

1. Crossword puzzle

Pupils make crossword puzzles starting with their first names or their first names and their surnames.

1. Each pupil writes his/her name down on a sheet of paper (squared paper is best), as shown in the example.
2. He/She adds his/her favourite food, hobbies, colours, personal characteristics, etc. to the letters.
3. She/He draws the outline of the puzzle on a new sheet of paper and numbers the words.
4. Clues are added at the bottom of the sheet. Pupils can also draw pictures as clues, of course. For example:
   1. *My favourite colour is …*
   2. *Something cold, which I like to eat in summer.*
5. Pupils exchange puzzles with a partner and try to complete their partner's crossword.

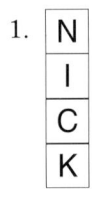

2. Holiday survey – Find someone who …

This is a communication game which the whole class can 'play'. Make copies of the pre-prepared questionnaire below or ask pupils to work in groups and make up 10 questions of their own to ask other members of the class. The questions must be about how members of the class spent their holidays. In either case, before pupils begin filling in their questionnaires, make sure they can build questions correctly in the past tense using one or two of the examples from the questionnaire below.

Pupils then move around the classroom asking each other the questions and answering them in the past tense. They should make a note of their results on their sheets. They should continue to ask different pupils in the class until they have filled in a name next to every item. When pupils have finished interviewing each other they should take it in turns to report back to the class what they have found out. For example: "*Some pupils in our class didn't spend their holiday in Europe. Nicholas went to Thailand. Simone went to Singapore and …*"

FIND SOMEONE WHO …	Names:
… went on holiday by plane.	
… stayed at home.	
… did not spend his/her holidays in Europe.	
… spoke English in the holidays.	
… learned a lot for school.	
… did not spend his/her holidays with their families.	
… only had good weather on holiday.	
… stayed on a camping site.	
… had a summer job.	
… went to the beach almost every day.	
… had an unusual experience on holiday.	
… was ill in the holidays.	

About Labor Day in the USA (1st Monday in September)

In the USA the first Monday in September is a national holiday. There are only five national holidays in the USA which are celebrated in all the states. These are: Thanksgiving Day (4th Thursday in November), Christmas Day (25th December), New Year's Day (1st January), Independence Day (4th July) and Labor Day. Labor Day is the American version of the European May Day or Labour Day and honours America's workers. Whereas May Day in Europe is at the beginning of the summer, Labor Day in the USA is a kind of "sending off" of the summer. Traditionally Labor Day is the last day of the summer holidays before going back to school. People usually celebrate by having barbecues, picnics or country fairs.

Song: Wonderful World

This song from the fifties was made popular by Sam Cooke who was born in 1935 and was tragically shot in 1964. *Wonderful World* has been sung by many other pop stars including Simon and Garfunkel. The original version sung by Sam Cooke is on the cassette. Unfortunately, in spite of repeated requests to the copyright holders, we were not granted permission to print the text of the song. However, the text is easy to understand. You may even find it in other popular songbooks which you may have.

Working with the song

<u>Before the 1st listening</u> tell pupils (possibly in pairs or groups) to write down the names of as many school subjects as they know.
<u>While listening</u> tell pupils to tick the subjects mentioned in the song which they also have on their lists and to try to add any new ones they hear.
<u>After the 1st listening</u> check the subjects pupils have noted down and those which are mentioned in the song. Then play the song again.
<u>After the 2nd listening</u> ask pupils whether they like the song or not and ask them to give reasons for their answers. Ask them what they think the song is really about. (Answer: *Love!*) Explain any new vocabulary.

Discussion

Write these questions on the board or an OHP and ask pupils to talk about them in groups and then report back to the class.
   1. Do you know any other school subjects?
   2. What are your favourite subjects at school? Why?
   3. Which subject do you like least? Why?

Project/Homework

Find out as much as you can about schools in Britain and the USA.

Discussion with older classes

Ask pupils to discuss the statements below in groups by making a list of arguments for and against. They should then report back to the class. They could then write their own opinions as a homework exercise.
   Do you agree or disagree with these statements? Give reasons.
   1. Most school subjects are a waste of time because they are not important later in life.
   2. My partner must be an 'A' student.

School is cool! – Copy master 1.1 (page 47)

On copy master 1.1 there are a number of humourous poems and rhymes which all have something to do with school. Copy the poems onto an OHP and present them to the pupils one at a time. (Either cut them out or cover them up appropriately.)

God made bees: Cover the word 'teachers' in the last line when presenting the poem. Ask pupils who they think 'we' are and what the missing word could be.

Writing Right: Before showing pupils the limerick ask them to write down the word 'right' correctly in as many different ways and with as many different meanings as they can. After reading and explaining the limerick ask pupils to try to find other English words which a) sound the same but are written differently (e.g. new and knew) and b) are written the same but have a different meaning or sound e.g. (football) match/match; to lead/lead.

Latin: You could use the rhyme as the start to a discussion about why pupils learn foreign languages at all – and of course in particular why Latin is still taught. (The discussion could take place in the mother tongue.)

Punctation Puzzle: Explain any new vocabulary and then tell pupils to put in commas and full-stops to make sense of the rhyme.

Solution: Ceasar entered, on his head
a helmet, on each foot
a sandal. In his hands he had
His trusty sword to boot.

School Dinners: Explain any new vocabulary. If your school has a canteen discuss the quality of the food there. Ask pupils what they (would) think of staying at school all day and having dinner together every day.

Chester: Before reading the poem ask pupils to give the three forms of various regular and irregular verbs, including come/say/grow and know.

It's School Today: Read the poem and then ask pupils the following questions:
What does the poem tell you about school in England?
When do you get up on school days?
Do you start school at the same time every day?
How do you get to school?
Are you always on time? Are you ever late?
Ask pupils to write a similar poem about their morning routine.

I love to do my homework: Before reading the poem ask pupils if they like doing homework or not! Ask them what they think of pupils who love doing homework (hopefully/probably eliciting the response from at least one pupil that these people are mad!). Finally hand the copy master out to pupils. They could choose their favourite poems/rhymes and learn them by heart as a homework exercise.

☆ Two poems for the first day of school – Copy master 1.2 (page 48)

These two poems are intended for use on the first day of school. Read the poems to the pupils and explain any new vocabulary using the illustrations for assistance. Ask pupils to carry out the tasks on the copy master and then discuss their answers with them.
Pupils could learn their favourite poem or at least one verse of "Summer goes" by heart.

The great school race – Copy master 1.3 (page 49)

This is a board game which can be played at the beginning of a school year or a term or at any time when school or the English school system is the topic in class.

Before playing the game make copies of the worksheet and stick them onto cardboard. To protect the games, you could also cover them with clear sticky-backed plastic.
The great school race is a game for 2-6 players. Each group needs a copy of the game board and a dice. Each player needs a counter (or spinner or coin).
Each player throws the dice in turn, moves his/her counter forward on the board and follows the instructions on the squares they land on.

Staying home from school – Copy master 1.4 (page 50)

On this worksheet there is an excerpt from Mark Twain's *Adventures of Tom Sawyer*. In order to allow pupils to read fluently, it is advisable to prepare a vocabulary list for your class explaining any new vocabulary. Hand this out with the text or preferably the day before and ask pupils to learn the vocabulary in advance.
Pupils read the text whilst listening to the cassette and carry out the True/False exercise on the copy master. The correct solutions are given on page 8.

Solution

STATEMENTS	True	False
1. Tom likes Monday mornings.		✗
2. That morning Tom wished he was sick.	✗	
3. One of his lower front teeth was loose.		✗
4. Tom had a sore finger.		✗
5. Tom groaned and woke up his sister Sid.		✗
6. Sid was worried about Tom.	✗	
7. Sid went downstairs and called their grandmother.		✗
8. Aunt Polly didn't believe that Tom's toe was mortified.	✗	
9. Tom told his aunt about his loose tooth.	✗	
10. Aunt Polly pulled his tooth out.	✗	
11. Tom didn't have to go to school that day.		✗

Further comprehension and discussion exercises
1. Describe the way Aunt Polly pulled Tom's tooth out.
2. Why did Tom feel quite happy at school after all?
3. How do you feel on Monday mornings?
4. Have you ever invented a story because you did not want to go to school?
   Write down/tell your story.

Further activity
In groups of four to six (Tom, Sid, Aunt Polly, Mary and Tom's school friends) ask pupils to write the extract as a play and act it out.

2 Autumn has come

The worksheets and activities in this chapter deal with autumn as harvest time and as a time of rainy and windy weather.

Autumn poems – Copy master 2.1 (page 51)

Present new vocabulary to your class before working with the copy master.

Homework: Read the poem to the class and ask the pupils to make a list of things which are typical of autumn and group them under the following headings: flora, fauna, weather, festivals. They should add any words of their own to the lists. Then tell pupils to build sentences using words on their lists. Finally ask pupils to write a short poem about autumn. It need not rhyme. (Guy Fawkes and Hallowe'en, which are mentioned in the poems are dealt with in detail on copy masters 3.2 and 3.3.)

Rain: This is a typical Silverstein nonsense poem! Ask pupils to practise reading the poem in groups, taking a few lines of it each to read. Tell them to decide facial expressions and actions which they could make to accompany their reading and then ask each group to perform to the class.

✱ Apple Harvest – Copy master 2.2 (page 52)

There are two recipes for desserts made with apples on this worksheet. The ingredients and instructions are listed on the copy master.
Whilst waiting for the desserts to cook you could play the following game.

Chain Game: I went to the greengrocer's ...

Play this simple chain game to practise the names of fruit and vegetables. Play the game as a class or preferably in groups of four to six.

Player A begins by saying: "I went to the greengrocer's and I bought some oranges."
Player B continues adding another item: "I went to the greengrocer's and I bought some oranges and a cauliflower."
Player C continues adding another item: "I went to the greengrocer's and I bought some oranges, a cauliflower and some potatoes."
The game continues like this with each player adding a new item to the list. If a pupil can't remember an item or can't think of a new item they are out and the chain begins again.

Song: Raindrops keep falling on my head

Music: Burt Bacharach, Text: Hal David
© 1969 by Blue Seas Music Inc./Jac Music Co. Inc. and 20th Century Music Corp., New York.

A
Raindrops keep fallin' on my head
And just like the guy whose feet are too big for his bed,
Nothin' seems to fit.
Those raindrops are fallin' on my head
They keep fallin'!

A
So I just did me some talkin' to the sun,
And I said I didn't like the way he got things done;
Sleepin' on the job.
Those raindrops are fallin' on my head,
They keep fallin'!

B
But there's one thing I know,
The blues they send to meet me
Won't defeat me.
It won't be long till happiness
Steps up to greet me.

A
Raindrops keep fallin' on my head,
But that doesn't mean my eyes will soon be turnin' red;
Cryin's not for me,
'Cause I'm never gonna stop the rain by complainin'.

C
Because I'm free – nothin's worryin' me.

This famous song by Hal David and Burt Bacharach is from the film "Butch Cassidy and the Sundance Kid".

First play the song to the class and ask them to note down how often they hear the title phrase 'Raindrops keep/ are fallin' on my head'. *(Answer:* 4 times)

Then write the second and third lines of each verse in the wrong order on an OHP and ask pupils to listen to the song again and put the text into the correct order.

Finally ask the pupils to summarise the verses in their own words or copy the summaries given below onto an OHP transparency. Then present them to the class in the wrong order and ask the pupils to decide which summary goes with which verse.

Finally ask pupils whether they like the song or not and sing the song with them.

Summaries

Verse 1: It is raining and the singer thinks that is the wrong type of weather because it doesn't match the way he is feeling. He thinks it is a bit like when someone is too big for the bed they are sleeping in.

Verse 2: The singer wants the sun to come out again and stop the rain. He tells the sun it should work harder and stop sleeping!

Verse 3: The singer won't let the bad weather make him unhappy.

Verse 4: The rain won't make the singer cry or be sad. And he won't complain about the weather because that won't stop the rain either. He is feeling good and has no worries. He doesn't mind the rain.

Weather wordsearch – Copy master 2.3 (page 53)

All the words in this wordsearch have something to do with the weather.

Individual activity: Pupils first find the hidden words in the puzzle and then complete the list on the worksheet in capital letters. Finally they use the letters marked to make a weather rhyme.

Group activity: Copy the puzzle onto an OHP transparency and present it to the class. Divide the class into teams of four students. Each team takes it in turn to come and circle one word. Set a time limit (e.g. 15 seconds) for finding the words. The team which finds the most words is the winner.

Solution

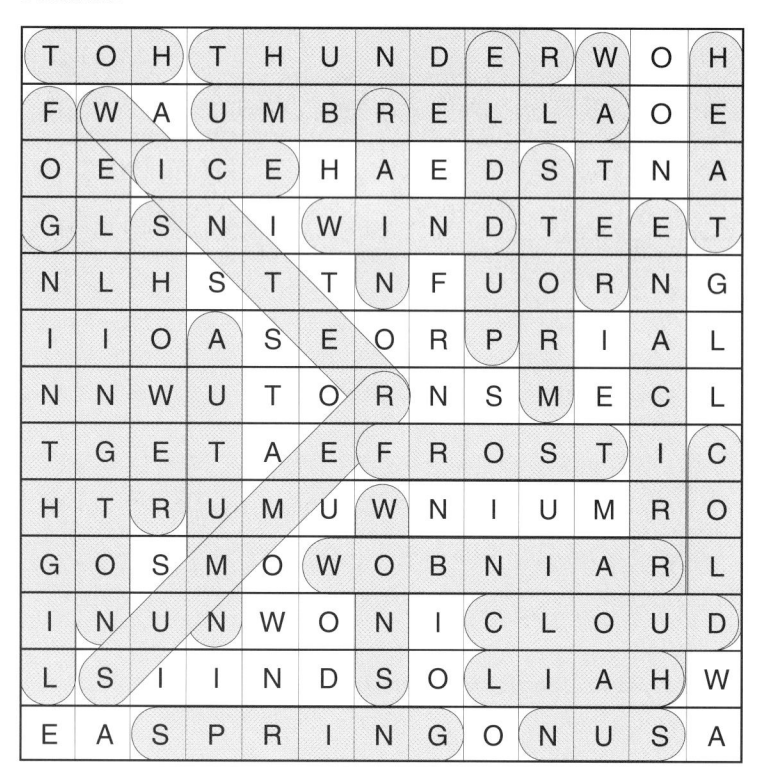

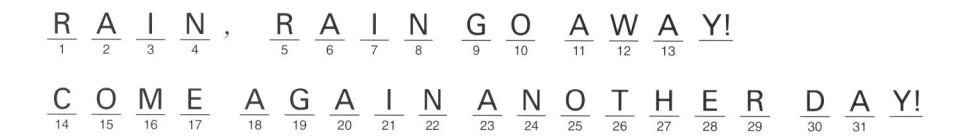

T	O	H	T	H	U	N	D	E	R	W	O	H
F	W	A	U	M	B	R	E	L	L	A	O	E
O	E	I	C	E	H	A	E	D	S	T	N	A
G	L	S	N	I	W	I	N	D	T	E	E	T
N	L	H	S	T	T	N	F	U	O	R	N	G
I	I	O	A	S	E	O	R	P	R	I	A	L
N	N	W	U	T	O	R	N	S	M	E	C	L
T	G	E	T	A	E	F	R	O	S	T	I	C
H	T	R	U	M	U	W	N	I	U	M	R	O
G	O	S	M	O	W	O	B	N	I	A	R	L
I	N	U	N	W	O	N	I	C	L	O	U	D
L	S	I	I	N	D	S	O	L	I	A	H	W
E	A	S	P	R	I	N	G	O	N	U	S	A

R A I N ,   R A I N   G O   A W A Y!
1 2 3 4   5 6 7 8   9 10   11 12 13

C O M E   A G A I N   A N O T H E R   D A Y!
14 15 16 17   18 19 20 21 22   23 24 25 26 27 28 29   30 31

10

A U T U M N   R A I N B O W
C L O U D   S H O W E R
C O L D   S N O W
F O G   S P R I N G
F R O S T   S T O R M
H A I L   S U M M E R
H E A T   S U N
H O T   T H U N D E R
H U R R I C A N E   U M B R E L L A
I C E   W A T E R
L I G H T N I N G   W E L L I N G T O N S
P U D D L E   W I N T E R
R A I N   W I N D

"That's the way the wind blows!" – Copy master 2.4 (page 54)

This copy master is about the wind as an important feature of our weather.

Phrases and expressions: Pupils should use dictionaries to find the meanings of the phrases and expressions given on the worksheet. They should then make sentences using the phrases and expressions to show that they have understood them.

Solutions

That's the way the wind blows. – *That's the way things are, there is nothing you can do about it.*
1. to get wind of something – *to hear about something, usually something secret*
2. to run like the wind – *to run very quickly*
3. to sail close to the wind – *to do something very risky, to nearly but not quite break a law or principle*
4. to take the wind out of somebody's sails – *to do or say something before somebody else can do or say it; to stop someone boasting about something by telling about it first*
5. to throw caution to the wind – *to ignore warnings, to be careless*
6. the winds of change – *a new way of living or being, an innovation*
7. He is full of wind. – *He talks in a meaningless way.*
8. There is something in the wind. – *Something unexpected is going to happen.*

❋ Wind and wind belts

A simplified explanation of how wind is created and about the world's "wind belts" is given on the copy master.

Pupils could: a) make a wall chart showing the world's wind belts as illustrated on the worksheet
                and/or
                b) design and label diagrams illustrating how wind is created.

3 Festivals in October and November

Song: We are the World

Music/Text: Michael Jackson and Lionel Richie
© 1985 by Mijac Music/Brockman music. All rights for Germany, Switzerland, E. Europe and CIS held by Neue Welt Musikverlag GmbH, Munich

There comes a time when we heed a certain call,
When the world must come together as one.
There are people dying and it's time to lend a hand
To life, the greatest gift of all.

We can't go on, pretending day by day
That someone, somewhere soon will make a change.
We are all part of God's great big family
And the truth, you know love is all we need.

We are the world, we are the children,
We are the ones who make a brighter day, so let's start giving.
There's a choice we're making, we're saving our own lives,
It's true we make a better day, just you and me.

Well, send them your heart so they know that someone cares
And their lives will be stronger and free.
As God has shown us by turning stone to bread,
So we all must lend a helping hand.

We are the world, we are the children,
We are the ones who make a brighter day, so let's start giving.
There's a choice we're making, we're saving our own lives,
It's true we make a better day, just you and me.

When you're down and out, there seems no hope at all.
But if you just believe there's no way we can fall.
Well, let us realize that a change can only come
When we stand together as one!

We are the world, we are the children,
We are the ones who make a brighter day, so let's start giving.
There's a choice we're making, we're saving our own lives,
It's true we make a better day, just you and me.

Listen to this song either around 24th October, which is United Nations Day, or on United Nations Universal Childrens' Day which is celebrated on the first Monday in October. This is the date recommended by the United Nations General Assembly, but in many countries the day is celebrated on a different date. (Pupils can try to find out when it is celebrated in their country.) Some information about these two days is given on page 13, and can be photocopied and handed out to the pupils.
The song *We are the world* was written in 1985 by Michael Jackson and Lionel Richie for United Support of Artists for Africa (USA for Africa), a non–profitable foundation which aims to fight hunger in Africa.
Play the song to the class and find out if any of the pupils know the song/who it is sung by/what it is about. Then explain any important new vocabulary to the class before playing the song again.
After the second listening ask pupils to work individually or in pairs and answer the comprehension questions below. Discuss their answers with them before asking them to go on to describe the message of the song. The discussion could take place as a class activity or in small groups with each group reporting back their ideas.

Questions about the song

1. According to the song, why is it time to help others?
2. Who can help? How?
3. What does the title mean?
4. Look at these key phrases from the song and use them to describe the message of the song.

| come together | it's time to lend a helping hand | love is all we need | we are the world | send them your heart |

Discussion

What can we do to help the poor and starving in the world?

☆ **Translation or reading exercise**

The text below deals with the same subject matter as the song and could be given to more able or advanced learners as a translation or reading exercise.

✻ **Africa's problems – our problems**

It is over 100 years since Africa was divided into colonies by the European States and now most African countries have become independent again. But there are still many problems, many of which are caused by the fact that there is not enough to eat or drink and because there are not enough medical supplies.

People in many parts of Africa earn very low wages, the economy in many African countries is very weak and the political systems are very unstable. There are serious environmental problems, large numbers of people cannot read or write, and although people die very young, the population is growing much quicker than in other places in the world. On top of all this, there is not enough rainfall and so the deserts are getting bigger and bigger. Unfortunately it is the poor, the weak and the least powerful who suffer the most: especially women and children. These people need help now in the form of food and medicine. But they also need long term agricultural and economic aid. We may not be able to solve their problems quickly, but we must try to help. We can't not try!

✻ **About United Nations Day and United Nations Universal Childrens' Day**

24th October is United Nations Day, a day which is dedicated to greater understanding and peace throughout the world.

The United Nations Organisation was established on 24th October 1945. Its aims were to maintain international peace and security, to develop friendly relationships between the different countries of the world and to encourage international co-operation so that the problems facing the world could be solved more easily.

United Nations Universal Childrens' Day is dedicated to children all over the world. It was established by the United Nations in order to encourage understanding and appreciation of children from all different ethnic groups. Officially the United Nations Universal Children's Day is celebrated on the first Monday in October, but many countries have decided to celebrate it on a different date. In Britain, for example, it is celebrated on the 15th June and is known as World Children's Day.

✻ **Columbus Day and the discovery of America – Copy master 3.1** (page 55)

October 12th or the second Monday in October is Columbus Day in the USA.

This worksheet tells the story of Christopher Columbus and the discovery of America and gives some information about how Columbus Day is celebrated in the USA today. Pupils should read the text and do the True/False exercise given below. Either read the sentences to the pupils or copy the exercise onto an OHP transparency. Ask pupils to find the islands and countries mentioned on a modern map of the American continent. Ask them to explain why Columbus sailed west in order to find India.

Columbus Day – True/False exercise

Write T (true) or F (false) next to these statements.
1. Christopher Columbus set sail from Italy.
2. He wanted to find the sea route to India.
3. Columbus sailed across the Pacific Ocean.
4. The names of his ships were "Niña", "Pinta" and "Santa Lucia".
5. There were 77 men on board his ships.
6. The journey was long and difficult.
7. The crews made threats of mutiny.
8. Before dawn, on 12th October 1592, the ships landed on an island in the Bahamas.
9. Columbus called the island "San Salvador".
10. Columbus was happy to find an unspoiled world where the native people lived in grass huts.
11. Back home, the Spanish King and Queen were very pleased about Columbus' discovery.
12. Columbus believed that he had found the sea route to India. That is why the natives of America were called Indians.
13. On Columbus Day people in America remember the day Christopher Columbus reached an island in the Bahamas.
14. The biggest celebrations take place in San Francisco.
15. Columbus Day is an important event for the Hispano-Americans because the discovery of America was a success for King Ferdinand and Queen Isabella of Spain.

Solution

1. F (Spain) 2. T 3. F (Atlantic Ocean) 4. F (Santa Maria) 5. F (88) 6. T 7. T 8. F (1492) 9. T
10. F (disappointed) 11. T 12. T 13. T 14. F (New York) 15. F (Italian-Americans)

It's Hallowe'en – Copy master 3.2 (page 56)

Use this worksheet on or around Hallowe'en – 31st October.
The text below **About Hallowe'en** is recorded on the cassette. Questions on the text are printed on the copy master. Allow the pupils to listen to the text three times: Play it all the way through the first time. The second time stop the cassette at various points to allow pupils to make notes for their answers. Finally play it through a third time so that pupils can check their answers. As a further exercise you could ask your pupils to work in pairs and write their own text about Hallowe'en using the questions and answers as guidelines.

With more advanced groups you could make the text into a cloze text by leaving out key words and asking pupils to fill in the missing words as they listen to the text. They could then answer the questions as a reading comprehension exercise.

There is also a wordsearch on the worksheet which pupils can do individually. The solution is given below.

About Hallowe'en

31st October is known as Hallowe'en in Britain and America. It is a very popular and exciting occasion especially in America. On Hallowe'en you often see jack-o'-lanterns in the windows of people's houses and in doorways. Jack-o'-lanterns are hollowed-out pumpkins with grinning faces cut into them which are lit up by candles.

On Hallowe'en night there are often fancy dress parties. People dress up as witches and ghosts and other "spooky" characters and wear frightening masks.

It is also a widespread tradition, especially in America, for children to go from house to house playing "trick or treat". They knock on doors and the houseowners either have to give them a treat (money, sweets, cookies) or the children play a trick on them. Typical "tricks" are putting something horrible on the doorstep or smearing soap on the door handle. Unfortunately tricks are not always harmless fun. "Trick or treating" has been known to reach dramatic proportions, with dangerous and harmful tricks being played and poisonous treats being given.

Hallowe'en is in fact a very old festival which dates back to pre-Christian times. But although Hallowe'en has changed over the centuries it has always been associated with witches, ghosts and superstitions.

The Celts thought of this time as New Year's Eve because it marked the end of the summer and the beginning of a new year for them. The Celts believed that on this night evil spirits came to earth. Huge fires were lit to frighten these evil spirits away and people dressed up as ghosts and goblins in the hope that they would not be recognised by the spirits.

In Christian times this New Year's festival became known as Hallowe'en. On this day and the following two days, called All Saints' Day (1st November) and All Souls' Day (2nd November), Christians remember the Saints and all dead people.

Solution to wordsearch

A		I	J	N	S	O	S	D	A	X	A	D	V	T	K	P	V	J	U
O	H	C	T	F	F	A	L	L		S	A	I	N	T	S'		D	A	Y
C	D	N	M	U	Z	L	B	C	E	U	B	E	O	R	V	Q	R	C	A
T	G	C	A	N	D	L	E	S	C	P	D	E	V	I	L	U	M	K	P
O	N	A	R	E	V		B	P	E	E	F	U	S	C	D	Z	L		K
B	R	N	P	P	A	S	B	O	H	R	W	M	B	K	C	W	C	O'	H
E	F	D	C	U	C	O	E	O	H	S	R	A	J		G	I	T		I
R	H	Y	L	M	T	U	K	K	I	T	K	S	J	O	A	T	S	L	Z
Y	U	W	D	P	Q	L	X	Y	A	I	B	K	S	R	D	C	R	A	E
S	Q	G	F	K	L	S'	J	C	L	T	G	S	J		W	H	B	N	Q
P		O	P	I	M		L	L	A	I	K	I	E	T	H	E	P	T	F
I	V	B	D	N	U	D	Y	C	B	O	N	F	I	R	E	S	G	E	Y
R	O	L	V	S	Y	A	R	F	Z	N	Y	S	X	E	J	H	H	R	X
I	W	I	G	M	Z	Y	E	O	Y	T	W	T	X	A	L		K	N	A
T	B	N	D		N	O	P	M	Q	S	P	A	R	T	I	E	S	U	V
S	G	S	Q	G	H	O	S	T	S	M	X	R	W	N	M	N	F	X	

Activities for Hallowe'en

1. Spooky spellings

Pupils have to try to find words with silent letters in them, like the 'k' in 'knife' or the 'g' in 'reign'. They could collect the words on large paper ghosts and display them in the classroom.

2. Hubble, bubble, toil and trouble

Pupils may have played a game similar to this in their own language.
One pupil is the witch. She thinks of a rule by which she chooses other pupils or things to join her in her castle. She doesn't tell anyone her rule.
The pupils sit in a circle. The witch stands in the middle. In the example below the rule is that everyone must have an 'a' in their name.

Witch: Hubble, bubble, toil and trouble,   *Pupil A:* Hubble, bubble, toil and trouble,
         Fire burn and *Laura* bubble.   Fire burn and *Lucy* bubble.

The name Lucy hasn't got an 'a' in it so it doesn't comply with the rule. The witch shakes her head and Pupil A must stay in the circle and wait for another turn.
Now Pupil B takes over and repeats the rhyme putting in another name, for example, David. This complies with the rule so the witch tells the pupil to join her in the middle.
Now the next pupil in the circle takes over. Pupils must try to work out what the rule is. The pupils must not explain the rule even if they think they know it, they must simply repeat the rhyme choosing something which complies with the rule. If a pupil thinks they know, but it is not their turn they can put their hand up and have a try. The last pupil to be left sitting in the circle is the witch in the next round.

3. Talking about superstitions

Hallowe'en has always been associated with witchcraft, evil and superstition. So it is the ideal time to have a (critical) look at superstitions in class.

Find out whether: – pupils know any superstitions (in their countries).
                         – they know about the origins of these superstitions.
                         – pupils believe in any superstitions. Which ones?
                         – they know people who believe in superstitions. What kind of people are they?

These are some of the most common superstitions in Britain and America:
– 13 is an unlucky number.
– Friday 13th is an unlucky day.
– It is bad luck – to walk under a ladder.
              – to pass someone on the stairs.
              – to open an umbrella in the house.
              – to step on a crack while walking on the sidewalk.
              – if a black cat crosses your path.
– It is good luck to see a chimney sweep.
– If you break a mirror you will have bad luck for seven years.
– You can make a wish if you see a shooting star and it will come true.

4. A ghostly game!

This is a good party game, but you could play it in your class, too. Explain any new vocabulary from the 'story' before starting. You will need these objects: a dried apricot; two skinned grapes; a long, half-cooked, cold carrot; some long strands of wool soaked in cooking oil; a handful of cooked rice; cooked wet spaghetti; a banana cut in half and then cut lengthwise; a half-cooked, cold head of cauliflower.

Darken the classroom and tell pupils to sit in a circle with their eyes shut or better still wearing blindfolds.
Now tell them this story and pass around the things at the appropriate times.

The Captain's ghost

On the first journey to America there was a terrible storm and the captain of one of the ships was drowned. Now, each year on *(today's date)* parts of the captain's body come floating to the surface, and I have got them here for you.

Here is the captain's left ear. *(Pass dried apricot.)*
And here are the captain's eyeballs. *(Pass peeled grapes.)*
And here is the captain's middle finger. *(Pass carrot.)*
And here is the captain's hair. It's a little bit slimy. *(Pass wool.)*
And here are some maggots which were eating out his stomach. *(Pass rice.)*
And here are the captain's veins. *(Pass spaghetti.)*
And his tongue, the poor man. *(Pass banana.)*
And last of all – his brain. *(Pass cauliflower.)*

Guy Fawkes' Night – 5th November – Copy master 3.3 (page 57)

Hand out the worksheet and then play the cassette or read the text below to the pupils twice. They should follow the pictures whilst they are listening.
Then ask pupils to retell the story in their own words a) orally and b) in writing.

About Guy Fawkes' Night

The night of November 5th is not a good night for British cats, dogs and babies. On that night, in Britain, fireworks are let off in huge numbers and almost everyone gathers around large bonfires. Strange figures of a man made of old clothes, straw and paper burn on top of these fires. It is Guy Fawkes' Night, or simply Bonfire Night, in Britain.

On November 5th people in Britain remember Guy Fawkes' unsuccessful attempt to blow up the King and Parliament with 36 barrels of gunpowder on that night in 1605. Guy Fawkes was caught, taken to the Tower of London and later hanged for treason.

Since then November 5th has been celebrated in England with fireworks and huge bonfires. In the fortnight before November 5th children make large figures of Guy Fawkes out of old clothes. They stuff them with newspapers or straw. These figures are taken out onto the streets, and the children ask people passing by for a "Penny for the Guy". On November 5th, these Guys are burnt on the bonfires.

Thanksgiving – Fourth Thursday in November (USA) – Copy master 3.4 (page 58)

On the worksheet there is a cloze text about Thanksgiving Day, which is an important festival in the USA and is celebrated on the fourth Thursday in November. The text is recorded on the cassette.
Pupils can either fill in the words in the cloze text, then listen to the cassette to check whether they have put the words in the correct places, or complete the text while listening. There are also some comprehension questions on the copy master, which should be answered after the text has been completed.

Solution

Thanksgiving is celebrated in the USA on the *fourth* Thursday in November. It commemorates the first Thanksgiving in 1621 which was celebrated in *Plymouth*, New England by the Pilgrims, new settlers from England who had arrived there a year before.

The Pilgrims left Plymouth in England in September 1620 on their ship, the *Mayflower*. After a long and hard *voyage* they finally landed at a place on the North American coast, which they called Plymouth, New England. The first *winter* was very hard for the Pilgrims. They were not very good *farmers* and the plants and seeds they had brought with them did not flourish in the rough *climate* of New England. There was not enough *food*, the winter was hard and there were *diseases*. More than *half* of the settlers died.

In the second year the local Indian *tribes* helped the Pilgrims with their spring planting of native crops like *corn* and *sweet potatoes*.

After their first successful *harvest* that autumn they had a big Thanksgiving feast, together with the Indians who had helped them to *survive*.

Nowadays Thanksgiving is celebrated with colourful *parades*. The biggest one takes place along Central Park West in New York. But above all, Thanksgiving is a day for families to come *together*. There is usually a big *dinner* with *turkey*, corn, sweet potatoes and other vegetables and *pumpkin pie*.

4 Christmas is coming

Song: Another Rock and Roll Christmas

Text and music: Gary Glitter/Mike Leander/Eddie Seago
© by Morrison Leahy Music Ltd. Musik-Edition
Discoton GmbH (BMG UFA Musikverlage), Munich for
Germany, Austria, Switzerland, E. Europe and former Yugoslavia

(On Copy master 4.1 there is a lot of information about Christmas customs and it may be advisable to use this worksheet first.)

Intro: Christmas, Christmas, Christmas

A *Verse 1*
Light the lights, ring the chimes,
Come on in it's party time.
Raise a glass for Auld Lang Syne,
Come on and rock it up for all mankind.
Good to see friends I know
Kissing under the mistletoe.
I love to hear the children sing,
It looks like Santa's gonna bring …

B *Chorus 1*
Another Rock and Roll Christmas –
Another Christmas Rock and Roll!
Presents hanging from the tree,
You'll never guess what you got from me.
Another Rock and Roll Christmas –
Another Christmas Rock and Roll!
We better hold each other tight,
You never know it might snow tonight.

17

A *Verse 2*
Guys and girls, stay up late,
So excited they can't wait.
Let there be peace on earth,
Come on and rock and roll for all you're worth!
We're gonna laugh, we're gonna sing,
We're gonna make the rafters ring.
Pull my cracker, let me be,
The silver star upon your tree!

B *Chorus 2*
Another Rock and Roll Christmas –
Another Christmas Rock and Roll!
All dressed up, so here we go.
Do I hear sleigh bells in the snow?
Another Rock and Roll Christmas –
Another Christmas Rock and Roll!
Tonight Old Santa never, never stops:
He bops above the chimney tops.

C
And you'll be rocking in your stocking,
When you see your big surprise
'Cause I'll be rocking in your stocking
You won't believe your big, blue eyes.

A *Verse 3*
Come on in, join the fun,
It's Christmas time for everyone.
May your days be merry and bright,
This ain't gonna be no silent night.
See the stars glittering,
Soon they gonna see the New Year in.
No one's looking, kiss me quick,
Come on and rock and roll for Ole Saint Nick!

B *Chorus 1*   Christmas, Christmas, Christmas
B *Chorus 2*
B *Chorus 1*

1. Ask the pupils to list the typical features of Christmas in England which they hear about in the song. *These are:*
   – *having a party at Christmas*
   – *singing "Auld Lang Syne"*
   – *kissing under the mistletoe*
   – *Santa Claus (or Father Christmas) bringing presents*
   – *pulling Christmas crackers*
   – *Santa arriving on the roof in a sleigh (pulled by reindeer)*
   – *stockings (people hang up stockings for Father Christmas to put presents in)*

2. Ask pupils to make illustrations to go with the song. Their work could be displayed in the classroom.

Christmas: facts, fun and faith – Copy master 4.1 (page 59)

On this worksheet there is information about Christmas customs in Britain, the USA and Australia. Before reading the worksheet with the pupils, ask them to note down or tell you what they already know about Christmas in Britain and the USA. Questions and answers based on the information on the worksheet are given below. (Before pupils read the information tell them that they are going to do a quiz/you are going to ask them questions on it afterwards.)

Christmas Quiz

The questions and answers for this quiz are printed below. Ask the questions in any order or make up new questions according to what your group knows. Either ask the questions as a question/answer exercise or have a Christmas Quiz Team Game as described below.

Team Game

You will need a star (or any other "Christmassy" thing).
1. Divide the class into three teams.
2. Put the star on a table at the front of the classroom.
3. Ask the teams to line up at the back of the classroom with the first pupil in each team (the runners) standing the same distance away from the table with the star on it.
4. Read out a question. (Tick off the question on your list.)
5. The runners work out the answer – either by themselves or by asking fellow team members for help and using the worksheet – but must not call it out.
6. As soon as a runner knows the answer she/he runs to the front, and takes the star.
7. The runner with the star in his/her hand first can answer the question. If the answer is right the team gets one point. If it is wrong the other teams get one point each and the teacher gives the correct answer.
8. The runners return to the end of their team's line.
9. Now the next person in the line is the runner.
10. The team with the most points at the end is the winner.

Questions

1. What might you see in shops and banks in Britain before Christmas?
   Paper chains and balloons
2. What do people in Britain and the USA do with the Christmas cards they receive?
   Put them on the mantlepiece or hang them on the walls
3. When was the first Christmas card printed?
   In 1843
4. How many copies of the first Christmas card were printed?
   1,000
5. Who invented the first Christmas card?
   Sir Henry Coles
6. Sir Henry Coles was the director of a famous London museum. What is the museum's name?
   The Victoria and Albert Museum (V and A)
7. Who is the most popular producer of charity cards today?
   UNICEF
8. Where did the custom of decorating the Christmas tree come from?
   Germany
9. What do you often see on Christmas trees instead of candles?
   Fairy lights
10. What do carol singers often get for their singing?
    Money (often for charity)
11. What do young children write in their letters to Father Christmas?
    A list of the presents they would like to get
12. When do children in Britain and the USA get their Christmas presents?
    On Christmas Day
13. What animal pulls Father Christmas' sleigh?
    Reindeer
14. Why is the day after Christmas called Boxing Day?
    Because in earlier times churches had boxes which people could put presents or money for the poor into on Christmas Day. These boxes were opened the day after Christmas: Boxing Day.
15. What are the special plays called, which take place in British theatres at Christmas time?
    Pantomimes
16. What are the little pies called, which people in Britain eat at Christmas time?
    Mince pies
17. Which green plant do British and American people make wreaths out of at Christmas?
    Holly
18. When do English people have to kiss each other at Christmas?
    When they are standing under the mistletoe
19. Where do many Australian people have their Christmas dinner?
    On the beach
20. What do thousands of Australians do when they meet in city parks on Christmas Eve?
    Sing Christmas carols

The Giant Christmas Crossword – Copy master 4.2 (page 60)

Pupils should have a good knowledge of Christmas customs and vocabulary before doing the crossword.
(For information see copy master 4.1 and/or the information given in *Around the Year 1* – Klett order number: 512741 pp. 30-32)

Solution

Across: 4. pantomime 6. reindeer 7. Santa 9. balloons 12. crackers 13. holly 16. tree 18. fairy 19. wrapping 21. Claus 23. star 24. bell 25. ribbon 26. mince 27. lights 28. pies 29. wreath
Down: 1. candle 2. stocking 3. crib 4. presents 5. mistletoe 8. turkey 10. cake 11. decorations 12. carol 14. Christmas 15. bauble 17. angel 20. tinsel 21. cards 22. sleigh

Christmas jokes – Copy master 4.3 (page 61)

This copy master is 'just for fun'. You may have to explain the punchline of some of the jokes. Pupils may want to learn their favourite joke by heart and tell it to a friend or a classmate. They can also use the jokes in crackers, if they make some. (See copy master 4.4)

✱ Christmas crackers – Copy master 4.4 (page 62)

This copy master gives information about and instructions for making Christmas crackers. The material needed is given on the worksheet.

Song: Last Christmas

Music/Text: George Michael
© 1984 by Morrison Leahy Music Ltd. All rights for Germany, Switzerland, E. Europe and CIS held by Chappel & Co. GmbH, Hamburg

[Musical score with lyrics:]

Last Christ-mas I gave you my heart. But the ve-ry next day you gave it a-way. This year to save me from tears I'll give it to some-one spe-cial..... ...Once bit-ten and twice shy, – I keep my dis-tance, but you still catch my eye. Tell me ba-by, do you re-cog-nise me? Well it's been a year, it doesn't sur-prise me.

A
Last Christmas I gave you my heart.
But the very next day you gave it away.
This year to save me from tears
I'll give it to someone special. *(twice)*

B
Once bitten and twice shy, –
I keep my distance, but you still catch my eye.
Tell me baby, do you recognize me?
Well, it's been a year, it doesn't surprise me.

B
Happy Christmas – I wrapped it up and sent it
With a note saying "I love you", I meant it.
Now I know what a fool I've been.
But if you kissed me now,
I know you'd fool me again.

A   *(twice)*

B
Crowded room – friends with tired eyes,
I'm hiding from you and your solemn eyes.
My God I thought you were someone to rely on.
Me, I guess, I was a shoulder to cry on.

B
A face on a lover with a fire in his heart.
A man undercover, but you tore him apart.
Ooh, ooh, now I've found a real love.
You'll never fool me again

A   *(twice)*

B
A face on a lover with a fire in his heart.
A man undercover, but you tore him apart.
Maybe next year I'll give it to someone,
I'll give it to someone special, special, someone …

This song is played frequently on the radio every Christmas in Britain. Play the song to the pupils and ask them to answer the questions below.

Questions on the song

1. What did the singer give his girlfriend last Christmas? Was it a 'real' present?
2. What do you think he means when he says she gave his heart away?
3. What is the singer going to do this year?
4. He notices his ex-girlfriend, but does she notice him? How do you know?
5. Could he fall in love with her again? How do you know?
6. Has the singer found a new girlfriend yet? How do you know?
(7. Write the story of the song in your own words, as if it was a letter from the singer to the girl.)

Further activities

Writing tasks.
Write about 100 words on one of these subjects:

1. Christmas in my family.
2. The best Christmas I have ever had.
3. Christmas – no thanks!

Christmas with a difference

1. Christmas in the past: Find out from your grandparents what Christmas was like when they were your age. In class decide on a set of questions, so that everybody asks the same questions. (Ask the questions in the language of the person you are interviewing.) Write down the answers in English. Report back your findings to the class.
2. Christmas in other countries: Are there any pupils from other countries in your class? Find out about how Christmas is celebrated in other countries or whether it is celebrated at all.

Games

Once Christmas was the only time of the year when games were allowed to be played! Playing games at Christmas either at Christmas parties or after Christmas dinner is still very popular in Britain.

Word games

1. **Christmas alphabet:** Find a Christmas word for each letter of the alphabet.
   (Work in pairs/teams; set a time limit; see who has finished first.)
2. **Christmas words:** How many words can you make out of the word CHRISTMAS?
   (Work in pairs/teams; set a time limit; see who has finished first.)
3. **Scrambled Christmas:** Write Christmas words in scrambled letters on the board and see who/which team can unscramble them first.
4. **Santa's reindeer – a chain game:** Players must think of an adjective to describe Santa's reindeer. Each new adjective must begin with the next letter of the alphabet. Limit the time a player has to think of a new word (by counting to ten, for example). A player who cannot think of a word in time or forgets one of the other words is out.
   Example:
   Player A: "Santa's reindeer is an active reindeer."
   Player B: "Santa's reindeer is an active, beautiful reindeer."
   Player C: "Santa's reindeer is an active, beautiful, crazy reindeer."
   Here are some examples for "difficult" letters: jellyfish-eating, qualified, queer, vandalizing, volleyball-playing, xylophone-playing, Xmas-loving, yellow, yoga-practicing, zigzag-running, zoo-hating.

Find your partner

The object of the game is for players to find out who/what they are and then find their partners.

1. Ask pupils to think of people and things that go together.
   For example: Romeo+Juliet; ham+eggs; bread+butter; tea+milk; Robinson+Friday; Laurel+Hardy; salt+pepper; fish+chips.
2. Write one half of each 'partnership' on one piece of paper and the other half on a different piece of paper.
3. Stick one piece of paper on each of the players' backs without telling them who they are.
4. Players walk around and ask each other 'Yes/No' questions in order to find out who they are.
   For example: Am I something to eat? Am I famous? Am I still alive? Am I a person? Am I a man?
5. When they have found out who they are they must find their 'partners'.

Who is finished first/last?

5 New Year and winter

Nick's thank you letter – Copy master 5.1 (page 63)

This worksheet should be used on the first day of school after the Christmas break. Point out to pupils that it is very common in Britain to write a thank you letter to all the people who gave you presents at Christmas. There is a coded thank you letter on the copy master. After pupils have written down the proper letter, which is given below, they can write their own coded (thank you) letters for their partners to read.

Solution

> Dear Aunt Jane,
>
> Thank you* very much for the snakes and ladders* game which you sent me for Christmas. It is very nice. Rosemary and I played it for hours on Boxing Day. Next time you come to visit us, we can play it together. I hope to see you soon.
>   Love
>   Nick

* ewe = you
* Snakes and ladders is a boardgame which is very popular in Britain.

Further activity for New Year

New Year is a time for reflecting on things gone by and making new starts. In many countries it is popular to make New Year's resolutions for the coming year. Talk about New Year's resolutions in class. Use the following phrases: *I've decided to …/I've decided not to …/I'm going to …/I've made up my mind to … + start/give up/try*, etc.

Hogmanay – the Scottish New Year – is an important festival in Scotland. The following text gives background information about Hogmanay and can be photocopied and given to the pupils.

About Hogmanay – New Year in Scotland

In Scotland, Hogmanay, or New Year, is one of the most important celebrations of the year. Families, friends and relatives come together, and Scottish treats are served, such as shortbread, scones, Hogmanay oat crackers or black buns – dark buns filled with raisins, nuts and spices.
People go "first-footing": they visit friends and relations after midnight on Hogmanay and try to be the first person to enter the house through the front door. Some people still believe in the old superstition that their luck for the coming year is determined by the first person who enters their home as soon as the New Year has begun: If this "first footer" is a dark-haired man carrying a piece of coal, some bread and some salt (for warmth, hospitality and health), the house is supposed to have luck and good fortune in the New Year.

☆ HAPPY "CHINESE" NEW YEAR! – Copy master 5.2 (page 64)

A lot of Chinese people live in Britain and the USA. For them Chinese New Year is the most important festival of the year. You could use this worksheet when discussing Britain and America as multiracial societies.
Ask pupils to read the information about the Chinese calendar at the top of the worksheet. Then tell them to complete the lists of years in the Chinese calendar and find out about the years their parents, friends, and they themselves were born. Ask pupils to talk or write about the characteristics associated with the different animal signs and about the signs in general.
The information about Chinese New Year below can be (copied and) given to the pupils before or after handing out the worksheet.

☆ **About Chinese New Year**

As the Chinese follow a lunar calendar, the date of the Chinese New Year (Yuan Tan) is determined by the phases of the moon. It may fall anywhere between the middle of January and late February. It is the most important festival in the Chinese calendar. It lasts 15 days and it is celebrated by Chinese communities all over the world.
For Chinese people the end of the old year is the time for paying off debts, bringing accounting-books up-to-date and cleaning the house. The latter is especially important for them because they believe that evil spirits must be dusted away or swept out of the house and that bad luck must be washed away. Homes, offices and factories are decorated with branches full of flowers, flowers of prosperity, and red decorations with New Year messages on them.
A lot of food has to be prepared in advance because it is considered to be bad luck to use a knife or any other sharp instrument on the first days of the New Year.
Celebrations begin on New Year's Eve. New Year's greetings written on red paper are posted on doors and windows. Greeting cards are exchanged. People have a big dinner, and late in the evening, there is a firework display.

New Year's Day is a family day. People put on their best clothes to visit friends and family. Children receive little parcels of sweets wrapped in red paper and good luck money in red envelopes. The people eat festive food, such as New Year's pastry filled with nuts and fruit, rice pudding, rice dumplings and vegetarian dishes.

People spend the first days of the New Year meeting friends and relatives, or visiting temples, museums or places of entertainment. Most of the shops stay open, and there are open markets in many cities.

Two weeks after the start of Chinese New Year, on the fifteenth day of the first full moon, the Lantern Festival (Teng Chieh) takes place. Lanterns of all different colours, shapes and sizes are used to decorate the houses and streets. There are fantastic parades in the streets which are led by dragon or lion dancers. The dragon or lion is made of a framework of bamboo covered with silk or paper. Supported by a team of dancers it weaves its way up and down the streets, accompanied by musicians and acrobats. The Lantern Festival ends with a big firework display. The biggest parades in English-speaking countries take place in Soho in London and in Chinatown in New York and San Francisco.

Song: Winter Wonderland

Music: Felix Bernard, Text: Dick Smith
© by Bregman, Vocco & Conn., Inc., USA. Rights for Germany, Austria, Switzerland and E. Europe held by: EMI Music Publishing Germany GmbH

This song is an ideal song to play and sing on a really "wintry" day.

A
Sleigh bells ring, are you list'nin'!
In the lane snow is glist'nin';
A beautiful sight,
We're happy tonight,
Walkin' in a winter wonderland!

A
Gone away is the blue bird,
Here to stay is a new bird,
He´s singing a song,
As we go along,
Walkin' in a winter wonderland!

B
In the meadow we can build a snowman,
Then pretend that he is Parson Brown,
He'll say, "Are you married?" we'll say, "No, man!
But you can do the job when you're in town!"

A
Later on we'll conspire
As we dream by the fire –
To face unafraid,
The plans that we made,
Walkin' in a winter wonderland!

B
In the meadow we can build a snowman,
Then pretend that he's a circus clown.
We'll have lots of fun with Mr Snowman
Until the other kiddies knock him down.

A
When it snows ain't it thrillin'
Though your nose gets a chill in!
We'll frolick and play
The eskimo way
Walkin' in a winter wonderland!

✱ Snow – Copy master 5.3 (page 65)

Use this worksheet on a snowy day!

Baked Alaska is a popular American dessert. The ingredients needed are listed on the worksheet. It is very easy to make. If possible make it in the school kitchen in groups of 5-6 pupils.

Death of a snowman: Explain any new vocabulary to the pupils and then read the poem to them slowly. Ask them to answer the questions on the worksheet. Then ask them to practise reading the poem in pairs or groups of six with each reader taking one sentence of the poem in turn.
As an additional creative exercise ask pupils to write down the rhyming words from the ends of each line and then work in groups making a new poem using these words. You could also ask pupils to illustrate the different stages in the original poem.

Discussion
Would you rather live in an area with or without snow? Give reasons.

☆ ✱ Martin Luther King Day – Copy master 5.4 (page 66)

The third Monday in January is a national holiday in the USA. It commemorates Dr. Martin Luther King, the famous civil rights leader, and it celebrates his birthday which was on the 15th January. In 1964 Martin Luther King won the Nobel Peace Prize for his non-violent fight for social, political and economic equality for black Americans. During the fifties and sixties many Americans were involved in the civil rights movement which fought against laws and practises that discriminated against Afro-Americans.

The text about Martin Luther King below is recorded on the cassette and should be used as a listening comprehension exercise. The text does not appear on the worksheet but questions on it do. Play the cassette twice to allow pupils enough time to answer the questions on the worksheet. The answers are given below. After pupils have done the listening comprehension and you have checked their answers, play the text again. Then ask them to write their own text entitled About Martin Luther King.

About Martin Luther King

Martin Luther King was born on January 15, 1929, in Atlanta, Georgia. His father was a minister in one of Atlanta's leading black churches. At the age of 15, Martin Luther entered Morehouse College where he decided to become a minister like his father. He thought that in this job he would be able to help black Americans best. After college he went to Boston University. In 1947, he became a Baptist minister and later, pastor of a Baptist Church in Montgomery, Alabama. In 1953, he married Coretta Scott. They had four children together.
During the fifties Martin Luther King became a leader in the Civil Rights Movement. People committed to this movement fought against racial discrimination and for full civil rights for black people in the USA. Martin Luther King's first success in his fight against racial discrimination came when he organized a boycott of the buses in Montgomery, Alabama. A black woman had refused to give up her seat to a white passenger and had therefore been arrested. Martin Luther King led a 382-day boycott of the buses by black people.
On August 28, 1963, he led a march of more than 200,000 people in Washington, D.C. In front of the Lincoln Memorial he gave his now famous "I have a dream" speech. This is part of that speech:
"I have a dream that one day this nation will rise up and live out the true meaning of its creed: We hold these truths to be self-evident, that all men are created equal. (…)
"I have a dream that one day on the red hills of Georgia the sons of former slaves and the sons of former slave owners will be able to sit down together at the table of brotherhood. (…)
"I have a dream that my four little children will one day live in a nation where they will not be judged by the color of their skin but by the content of their character …"
Partly as a result of this demonstration, Congress passed the Civil Rights Act of 1964 and the Voting Rights Act of 1965. Racial discrimination in education, employment, voting, housing and in public places, such as theatres, restaurants, hotels, and sports stadiums was made illegal through these Acts.
Martin Luther King organized many marches and demonstrations. He believed in non-violent resistance to racial discrimination. All his life he fought for freedom and equality and against hate, prejudice and violence in spite of facing arrest and many other forms of trouble, like the bombing of his home.
In 1964, Dr. Martin Luther King was awarded the Nobel Peace Prize. He was the youngest person ever to win this prize.
On April 4, 1968, Martin Luther King was killed by a sniper in Memphis, Tennessee. The world was shocked by the news of his death. He was buried in Atlanta, Georgia. After his death more than 100,000 people attended his funeral and his wife, Coretta Scott King, continued the fight for civil rights.
In 1986, the third Monday in January was declared a national holiday to celebrate the birthday of Martin Luther King.

Answers
1. 15th January 1929 in Atlanta, Georgia 2. 15 years old, Morehouse College 3. Boston 4. Baptist minister 5. 1953, Coretta Scott 6. four children 7. Montgomery, Alabama 8. Montgomery, Alabama; boycott of the buses 9. march in Washington D.C., 200,000 people, famous "I have a dream" speech 10. Nobel peace prize 11. killed by a sniper in Memphis, Tennessee 12. national holiday to celebrate Martin Luther King's birthday

Song: Black, brown and white

Text/Music: Big Bill Broonzy

There's a little song that I'm singing about, People, you know it's true. If you're black and got to work for a living, This is, what they will say to you: Now, if you're white – you're alright, And if you're brown – stick around, But if you're black – oh brother, Get back, get back, get back.

A *Verse 1*
There's a little song that I'm singing about,
People, you know it's true.
If you're black and you got to work for a living
This is what they will say to you:

B *Chorus*
Now, if you're white _ you're alright,
And if you're brown – stick around,
But as you're black – oh, brother,
Get back, get back, get back.

A *Verse 2*
I was in a place one night,
They were all having fun.
There was all fine beer and wine,
But they would not sell me none.

B *Chorus*

A *Verse 3*
I went to an employment office,
I got a number and I got in line.
They called everybody's number,
But they never did call mine.

B *Chorus*

A *Verse 4*
Me and a man working side by side,
This is what it meant:
They was paying him a dollar an hour,
They was paying me fifty cents.

B *Chorus*

A *Verse 5*
I helped build this country,
And I fought for it too;
Now I guess that you can see
What a black man has got to do.

B *Chorus*

A *Verse 6*
I helped to win sweet victory,
With my little spade and hoe.
Now I want you to tell me, brother,
Whatcha gonna do about the old Jim Crow?

B *Chorus*

The song *Black, brown and white* was written by Big Bill Broonzy, a popular American blues singer who became famous during the 1930s. Big Bill Broonzy was born in 1893. His mother was once a slave and although he was brought up in a time when slavery had been abolished, black people were still discriminated against socially, economically, educationally and politically.
In his song Big Bill Broonzy describes various situations in which he was a victim of racial discrimination. The words printed may differ from the words which are sung on the cassette. This is not unusual because blues were not written down originally. Traditionally blues were kept alive through spontaneous improvisation.
Pupils should listen to the song. Explain any new words to them, then ask them to describe in their own words what happened to the singer: at the bar (verse 2), in the employment office (verse 3), and in his job (verse 4). Ask pupils to explain the meaning of the last two verses: namely that the singer finds it especially unfair that he is discriminated against in a society which he risked his life for in the war.

6 Festivals in February and March

The activities and worksheets in this chapter cover Valentine's Day (14th February); President's Day (third Monday in February), a public holiday in the USA when the birthdays of George Washington (22nd February) and Abraham Lincoln (12th February) are celebrated; Pancake Day (Shrove Tuesday, Carnival, Mardi Gras) which usually falls at the end of February; and St Patrick's Day (17th March), an Irish festival in honour of St Patrick, the patron saint of Ireland.

Song: When I'm sixty-four

Words/Music: John Lennon and Paul Mc Cartney
© copyright 1967 Northern Songs. Used by permission of Music Sales Limited. All rights reserved. International copyright secured.

A Verse 1
When I get older, losing my hair,
Many years from now,
Will you still be sending me a valentine,
Birthday greetings, bottle of wine?
If I'd been out till quarter to three,
Would you lock the door?
Will you still need me, will you still feed me,
When I'm sixty-four?

B
Hu …
You'll be older, too.
Ah, – and if you say the word
I could stay with you.

A Verse 2
I could be handy mending a fuse
When your lights have gone.
You can knit a sweater by the fireside,
Sunday mornings, go for a ride.
Doing the garden, digging the weeds;
Who could ask for more?
Will you still need me, will you still feed me,
When I'm sixty-four?

B
Ev'ry summer we can rent
A cottage on the Isle of Wight
If it's not too dear.
We shall scrimp and save.
Ah, – grandchildren on your knee,
Vera, Chuck and Dave.

A Verse 3
Send me a postcard, drop me a line,
Stating point of view.
Indicate precisely what you mean to say,
Yours sincerely, wasting away.
Give me your answer, fill in a form,
Mine for evermore.
Will you still need me, will you still feed me,
When I'm sixty-four?

Listen to this famous Beatles' song on or around Valentine's Day, 14th February. The word Valentine is mentioned in the first verse, line three, and refers to a Valentine card. After listening to the song ask pupils to answer the questions below.

Questions

Verse 1
1. How does the singer see himself in the first verse?
    He sees himself getting older and going bald.
2. What does he think his partner might do if he stays out late?
    He thinks she might lock the door so he can't get in!

Verse 2
3. What jobs around the house does the singer see himself doing?
    He sees himself mending fuses and doing the gardening.
4. How does he imagine his partner?
    He imagines her sitting next to the fire knitting a pullover!
5. What might they both do together on Sundays?
    They might go for a ride in their car or do the gardening.

Verse 3
6. What does the singer want his partner to do?
    He wants her to write him a letter saying how she feels about him.
7. What does he hope her message will say?
    He hopes she will say that she will marry him.

Further discussion

How is the man's and the woman's role in a partnership/marriage portrayed in this song?
Are these role models still valid today?
Do you agree with them? Why? Why not?
Could you see yourself in a similar relationship when you are old? Why/Why not?

14th February – Valentine's Day – Copy master 6.1 (page 67)

The following text about Valentine's Day is recorded on the cassette and can be used as a listening comprehension exercise. Play the cassette once to the pupils before they look at the questions. Then play the cassette again and ask them to answer the 18 questions on the worksheet. As there are so many questions you may want to ask pupils to work in groups. You could allocate a specific set of non-consecutive questions for each (group of) pupil(s) to answer. For example one group answers questions 1, 4, 7, 10, 13 and 16. The next group answers questions 2, 5, 8, 11, 14 and 17. The third group answers questions 3, 6, 9, 12, 15 and 18. When the pupils have finished, ask them to report back their answers to the class and then write their own text about Valentine's Day customs in Britain and America. They should make comparisons with Valentine's Day customs in their own country.

Solution: Listening Comprehension

1. *He is the patron saint of lovers.*
2. *In the third century AD*
3. *Both of them died on 14th February (on the eve of one of the most important Roman festivals, the Lupercalia)*
4. *It was an important Roman fertility festival.*
5. *Lots were drawn to find a partner: the names of young girls were put into a box and drawn out by young men. The girl the young man picked became his partner for a whole year.*
6. *In the 14th century*
7. *Presents were left anonymously. People who received presents had to find out who they were from. Sometimes the presents were more precious than Christmas presents.*
8. *Queen Victoria*
9. *During the second half of the 19th century (1837-1901)*
10. *In the 1930s*
11. *Hearts, roses, lace, rings, doves, Cupid*
12. *The Roman Goddess of love*
13. *Venus's son*
14. *People pierced by his magical arrows fell in love.*
15. *Messages and rhymes*
16. *Soon after the first settlers had arrived*
17. *They decorated their rooms with hearts, made Valentine cards and embroidered hearts.*
18. *It brightened up the cold winter days. It was a chance to visit friends, relatives and neigbours, and to have parties and think about love and romance!*

Solution to Valentine wordsearch:

G	I	F	T	A	V	E	W	O	C	A	R	D	S	A
I	B	L	Z	H	A	H	J	R	G	R	J	F	W	H
C	H	O	C	O	L	A	T	E	T	R	S	Y	E	U
U	Y	W	N	D	E	S	L	D	M	O	Q	Z	E	P
P	R	E	S	E	N	T	S	B	S	W	E	E	T	S
I	E	R	C	G	T	U	V	L	L	O	Z	D	H	G
D	N	S	M	R	I	B	B	O	N	A	P	O	E	M
K	X	R	D	J	N	F	K	V	P	N	V	U	A	L
I	C	L	A	C	E	I	H	E	A	R	T	Q	R	T
K	R	F	S	Q	X	T	E	P	R	O	C	V	T	B
D	A	R	L	I	N	G	A	R	I	N	G	A	E	W

About Valentine's Day

February 14th is Valentine's Day. Saint Valentine is said to be the patron saint of lovers. There were in fact two Roman saints with the name Valentine. One of them was an Umbrian bishop who died in 273 AD and the other was a Roman priest who died in 269 A.D. Both of them are said to have been put to death on February 14th. It is not clear why either of them should have become the patron saint of lovers. Perhaps because they both died on the eve of one of the most important Roman festivals, the Lupercalia.

Lupercalia was a fertility festival in honour of the God Pan. One of the customs at this festival was for young men to choose their partners for a year by drawing lots. The names of young women were put into a box and it was shaken up. Each young man drew out a name. The young woman chosen became the young man's partner for the next year.

Valentine's Day has been celebrated in England since the 14th century. Up to the end of the last century it was a custom in some parts of Britain to leave presents at the front doors of friends or relatives. The presents were left anonymously, and the people who received them had to find out who the presents were from. In some areas of Britain these Valentine presents were more precious than Christmas presents.

Exchanging cards on Valentine's Day has been popular in Britain since the 18th century and was particularly popular in the second half of the 19th century during the reign of Queen Victoria (1837-1901). After her reign it became less popular to send cards but the tradition was taken up again in the 1930s and is more popular than ever today. Typical pictures which used to be featured on Victorian cards are still popular today: hearts, roses, lace, rings, doves, which were said to be the favourite bird of Venus, the Roman goddess of love, and Cupid, Venus's son, who made people fall in love by piercing them with one of his magical arrows. Many cards have messages or short sentimental rhymes in them. Cards are traditionally sent anonymously.

In North America the tradition of celebrating Valentine's Day started soon after the first settlers had arrived. In the period before Valentine's Day, people made Valentine cards and embroidered hearts which they gave away as presents. They decorated their rooms with strings of hearts. Then, on Valentine's Day, people visited friends and relatives to deliver their Valentine's gifts and cards. In this way Valentine's Day brightened up the cold winter days for the early settlers. It was a good chance to have parties, meet other people and think about love and romance!

Further activities

1. Valentine letters

Ask the pupils to make as many words as they can using the letters in the word Valentine.

2. Mending broken hearts

Ask pupils to draw eight hearts on a sheet of paper and draw a line diagonally across each heart. Then tell them to write compound nouns on the hearts, with one half of each word on each side of the line. Pupils cut the hearts in half along the line. Then they give their 'broken hearts' to their partner and try to mend their partners' broken hearts.

Here are some examples of compound nouns which pupils could use: sunset, teaspoon, teapot, homework, blackbird, policewoman, busstop, fireworks, football, toothbrush, hairdresser, birthday, snowball, friendship.

3. Scrambled Valentine words

Pupils write scrambled Valentine words on a sheet of paper. Their partners must unscramble them.
Example: elvo = love
Here are some suitable words: arrow, cupid, lace, flowers, present, heart, darling, sweetheart, valentine, red, poem, gift, ring, ribbon, card, sweets, chocolates, dove.

✳ President's Day – Copy masters 6.2a and 6.2b (pages 68/69)

On President's Day people in the USA honour two of their greatest presidents: Abraham Lincoln (born on the 12th February) and George Washington (born on 22nd February). President's Day is celebrated on the third Monday in February.
Pupils should read the texts on copy master 6.2a and then complete the exercise on copy master 6.2b. They should use dictionaries to help them with any new vocabulary.

Solution to copy master 6.2b - Washington or Lincoln?
(W = George Washington, L = Abraham Lincoln):
1. W 2. L 3. L 4. W 5. W 6. L 7. W 8. L 9. W 10. L 11. W 12. W 13. L 14. W 15. L 16. L 17. L 18. W 19. L 20. L

Pancake Day – Copy master 6.3 (page 70)

The text below is recorded on the cassette. It is printed on the worksheet in scrambled form. Pupils have to unscramble the text on the worksheet after they have listened to it. They could mark the text on the worksheet in four different colours before copying it out in the correct order.

Shrove Tuesday
Shrove Tuesday is the last Tuesday before Lent, the forty days leading up to Easter. Why is it called Shrove Tuesday? Because, on the day before the beginning of Lent, people used to go to church to confess all the things they had done wrong and ask God to forgive them. This was known as "shriving", and "shrove" comes from shriving.

Pancake Day
Shrove Tuesday is also popularly called Pancake Day. This is because in the Middle Ages Lent was a time of fasting and people were not allowed to eat rich food, such as fat, eggs or milk until Easter. So, the day before Lent began, people used up all the eggs, fat and milk they still had in the house by making pancakes.
Today people in Britain traditionally eat pancakes with lemon juice and sugar on Pancake Day, though pancakes are rarely eaten at any other time of the year! Pancake races are held in several places in England on Pancake Day. The most famous race takes place in Olney, a village in Buckinghamshire, and this tradition is more than 500 years old. According to the rules all competitors must live in the village. They must wear aprons and have hats or scarves on their heads. They gather in the village square, each one holding a frying pan with a cooked pancake in it. When the Pancake Bell is rung they start running in the direction of the parish church. The pancakes have to be tossed three times during the race before they reach the church. If a pancake lands in the road, the racer is allowed to pick it up and toss it again! It is uncertain whether the pancakes are eaten at the end of the race!

Carnival
The word "carnival" comes from the Latin "carnem levare" which means "to take away meat". And in the past Christian people gave up eating meat during Lent because they believed that Jesus did not eat at all during this time. Carnival was a time for having fun before the forty days of fasting and prayer began. All sorts of games were played in the streets to celebrate. In many countries nowadays it is a time for dressing up in masks and costumes and having parties and dancing. In some countries the celebrations start at the beginning of January and last until Ash Wednesday, the first day of Lent.
Two of the most famous carnivals in the world are Rio Carnival in Rio de Janeiro, Brazil, and Mardi Gras in New Orleans. In Quebec City, Canada, the winter carnival celebrations last eleven days. They include parades and special sporting events, such as skating, skiing, tobogganing and canoe races through the freezing waters of the St. Lawrence river. Carnival, as such, is not celebrated in Britain.

Mardi Gras
New Orleans on Louisiana's Gulf coast is famous for its Mardi Gras celebrations. Mardi Gras is French and means "Fat Tuesday". And the festival was introduced there by the French colonialists.
People from all over the world go to New Orleans to celebrate Mardi Gras. There are parades and everyone dances in masks to the sound of jazz bands. Local specialities are sold in the streets: oysters, crabs, deep-fried sweet pastries and gumbo, a typical Creole dish. It is a thick bitter-sweet tasting soup made of shellfish, okra, onions, herbs and hot pepper.

Paddy's Green Shamrock Shore – Copy master 6.4 (page 71)

This is a song for St Patrick's Day, March 17th, which is celebrated in Ireland and everywhere in the world where Irish people live.

Paddy's Green Shamrock Shore is a song about emigration from Ireland, which is still a phenomenon (and problem) of life in Ireland today. The song is a traditional song from the days of the Great Famine (in the 1840s) when many Irish people died and many people had to leave their mother country. Most of them emigrated to America. The information below about St Patrick's Day can be given to the pupils before or after listening to the song.

Allow pupils to listen to the song first without seeing the text. Ask them to try and tell you what the song is about in a few words. Then hand out the text and play the song for a second time. Pupils should now underline words they do not understand. You can explain these or ask them to look them up in a dictionary. Then ask pupils to answer the questions on the worksheet. The answers are given below. Finally talk about emigration today. Are there any pupils in the class who have emigrated from other countries? Pupils should try to give reasons why people emigrate from their home countries today.

Solution to questions

1. *He left from Derry on 23rd May.*
2. *They were nice/pleasant.*
3. *They were heading for New York.*
4. *He wanted to go back to Ireland and marry the girl he left behind there.*
5. *All of the men were seasick.*
6. *There was no-one there to look after them.*
7. *The journey took 23 days.*
8. *They had a drink together because they didn't know if they would ever see each other again.*
9. *Possible headings: Verse 1: Bound for America; Verse 2: The passage; Verse 3: The arrival; Chorus: Farewell to Ireland*
10./11. a) and b) See pupils' own solutions.

> **About St. Patrick's Day (17th March)**
> On St Patrick's Day Irish people at home and abroad remember St Patrick, Ireland's patron saint.
> People wear green clothes and many of them wear a bunch of shamrock. The shamrock is a three-leaved plant which is the national emblem of Ireland. It is believed that St Patrick used the shamrock to illustrate the idea of God being three beings in one. St Patrick is a catholic saint and on St Patrick's Day people in the Republic of Ireland traditionally go to church in the morning and attend huge parades in the afternoon.
> Nowadays St Patrick's Day has become a celebration of Irish culture all over the world, especially in the USA, where lots of people of Irish origin now live.

7 Spring

These activities can be used at the end of winter and the beginning of spring.

The long winter – Copy master 7.1 (page 72)

Before working with this text ask pupils what spring means to them. Find out what they associate with spring.
On copy master 7.1 there is an extract from the book *The Long Winter* by Laura Ingalls Wilder. The text is recorded on the cassette. Pupils should read the text whilst listening and then carry out the tasks on the worksheet. Access to a map of the USA might be useful. You should prepare a vocabulary sheet explaining new words or make sure that dictionaries are available for pupils to use.
The story provides a good opportunity to introduce the litarary term "setting" meaning place and time of action.

Solution to the tasks

1. A blizzard is a snowstorm and the Chinook a warm, spring wind that comes down off the eastern slopes of the Rocky Mountains.
2. The story could be taking place at the end of the last century or beginning of this century. Trains are mentioned. There is no electricity and no central heating. The bedrooms are not heated. The kitchen is the only warm room in the house. The people have an open fire. They use twisted hay as fuel.
3. The story takes place at the end of March and in April.
4. The story takes place on the American prairie. The Chinook is mentioned, so it must be in one of the countries east of the Rocky mountains (see also question 1). The family is grinding wheat and twisting hay to use it as fuel so it must be taking place in the American wheat belt, possibly in Kansas, Oklahoma, Nebraska, Iowa, or Illinois.
5. People have to face the following difficulties in winter:
   – They are cut off.
   – There is no food and fuel.
   – It is cold and dark.
   – There are storms.
   – There is no school.
   These features of the end of winter are mentioned:
   – it gets warmer
   – trickling of water, dripping eaves
   – the Chinook

Song: Here comes the sun

Music/Text: George Harrison
© 1969 by Harrisongs Ltd. All rights for Germany, Austria, Switzerland and E. Europe held by Global Musikverlag, Munich

A
Here comes the sun, here comes the sun,
And I say, "It's alright."

B
Little darling, it's been a long cold lonely winter.
Little darling, it feels like years since it's been here.

A
Here comes the sun, here comes the sun,
And I say, "It's alright."

B
Little darling, the smile's returning to the faces.
Little darling, it seems like years since it's been here.

A
Here comes the sun, here comes the sun,
And I say, "It's alright."

C
Sun, sun, sun, here we come.   (repeat)

B
Little darling, I feel that ice is slowly melting.
Little darling, it seems like years since it's been clear.

A
Here comes the sun, here comes the sun,
And I say, "It's alright."

A
Here comes the sun, here comes the sun,
It's alright, it's alright.

Use this song and the poem on copy master 7.2 either as an introduction or follow-up to the story *The long winter* (copy master 7.1).
Ask pupils to listen to the song and try to work out the text by listening to it. Play the cassette often enough to allow pupils to write down the complete text. Then read out the text so that pupils can compare their texts to the original version.

Snowman – Copy master 7.2 (page 73)

Ask pupils to read the poem in groups with different pupils taking on each part. You need a narrator, pine trees, the snowman and a robin. Some pupils might want to illustrate the poem. You could ask pupils to carry out the (grammar) exercises below, which are based on the poem.

1. Find examples of the different tenses used in the poem.
   The following tenses are used: simple past/past continuous/future/conditional/present perfect/present simple
2. Make a list of the adjectives used in the poem.
   poor/sad/smiling/greatest/carrot/frosty/coal-black
3. Can you find any adverbs in the poem?
   bravely

✱ The first day of spring – Copy master 7.3 (page 74)

Use this worksheet on or around 21st March.
It can also be used in bilingual classes learning geography in English.
Before reading the text ask pupils to find out the time of sunrise and sunset on 21st March from a daily newspaper. Ask pupils what they notice. They should discover that day and night are of equal length on that day.
The solution to the diagram on the worksheet is given here.
Pupils could copy the diagram onto a large piece of paper and add typical pictures or photos illustrating the seasons in the northern hemisphere and in the southern hemisphere, too.

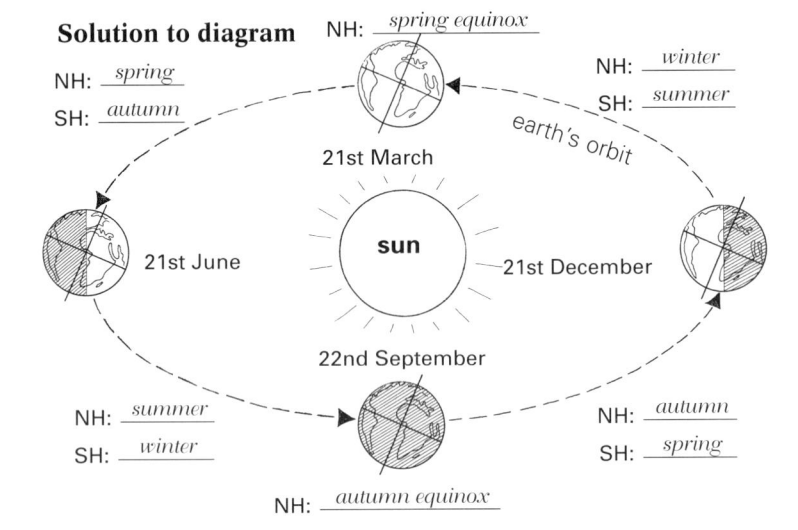

Solution to diagram

NH: *spring equinox*
NH: *spring*   NH: *winter*
SH: *autumn*   SH: *summer*
21st March
21st June — sun — 21st December
22nd September
NH: *summer*   NH: *autumn*
SH: *winter*   SH: *spring*
NH: *autumn equinox*

♪ Song: Garden song

music and text: David B. Mallet
© 1975 by Cherry Lane Publishing Company, Inc. All rights for Germany, Austria, Switzerland and E. Europe held by GLOBAL MUSIKVERLAG, Munich

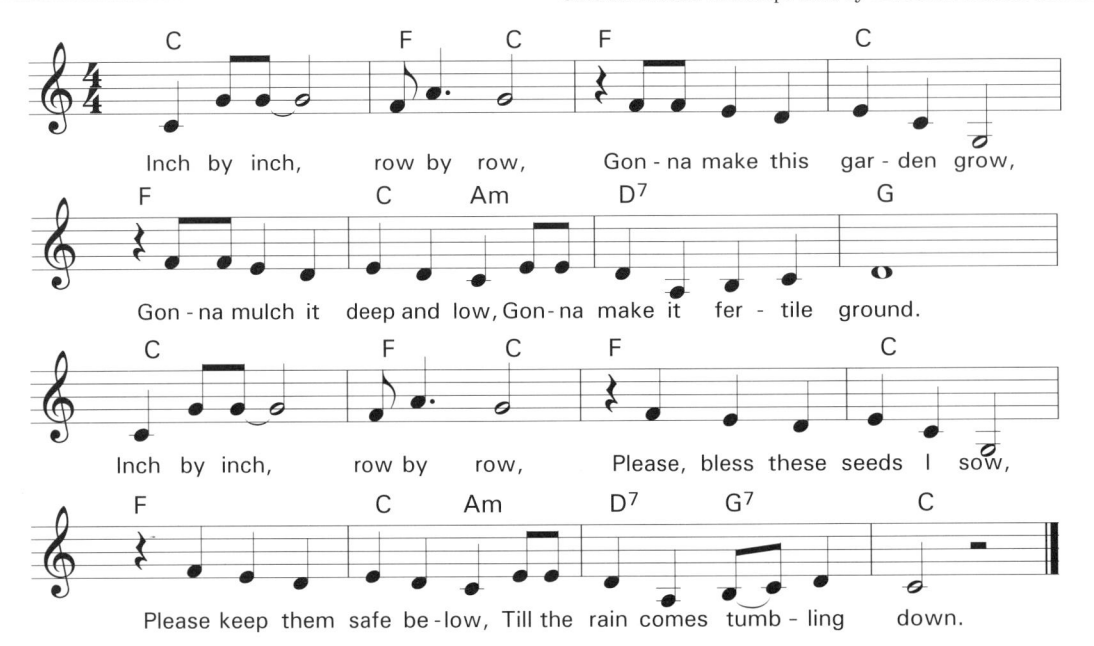

Inch by inch, row by row, Gonna make this garden grow,
Gonna mulch it deep and low, Gonna make it fertile ground.
Inch by inch, row by row, Please, bless these seeds I sow,
Please keep them safe below, Till the rain comes tumbling down.

Verse 1
Inch by inch, row by row,
Gonna make this garden grow,
Gonna mulch it deep and low,
Gonna make it fertile ground.
Inch by inch, row by row,
Please bless these seeds I sow,
Please keep them safe below
Till the rain comes tumbling down.

Verse 2
Pulling weeds, picking stones,
We are made of dreams and bones,
Need a place to call my own
'Cause the time is close at hand.
Grain for grain, sun and rain,
Find my way in nature's chain,
Tune my body and my brain
To the music of the land

(repeat verse 1)

Verse 3
Plant your rows straight and long,
Season with a prayer and song,
Mother Earth will make you strong
If you give her loving care.
Old crow watching from a tree,
He's got his hungry eye on me.
In my garden I'm as free
As that feathered thief up there.

(repeat verse 1)

This song is included here because spring is the time when people often start work in their gardens again after the winter. The *Garden Song* was made famous by the American folk singer, Arlo Guthrie.
Write the first half of each line of the song onto an OHP transparency. Cut each half line out into separate strips and place them in the wrong order on the OHP. Do not present them to your pupils at this stage. Without telling the pupils the title of the song or anything else about it, ask them to work out what the song is about while they are listening to it for the first time.
Then switch on the OHP and present the pieces of text you have prepared. Play the song again verse by verse. Stop the cassette at the end of each verse and ask different groups of 2 or 3 pupils to put the parts of the lines belonging to the verse they have just heard into the correct order.
Now ask pupils to copy down the incomplete verses into their exercise books.
Play the song again and ask pupils to try to complete the text.
Then play the song for a fourth time to allow pupils to check their versions with the version on the cassette.
Finally ask pupils to say how the writer feels when he is at work in his garden. Find out whether the pupils liked the song or not. Ask them to give their reasons.

✱ Gardens, gardening and land use - Copy master 7.4 (page 75)

Ask pupils to work in groups and carry out the survey on the worksheet. Tell them to report their findings back to the class.
There is also an extensive list of English names for flowers, herbs, vegetables and fruit on the worksheet. Pupils should again work in groups and look up the words in their own languages. They are then asked to group the words under the four headings: Flowers, Herbs, Vegetables and Fruit. As a further activity you could ask pupils to find out which season the various things grow in and group them under the headings for the seasons.

Further activities

Animals and their young

Make a transparency giving the English names of animals on the left, the names of their young in the incorrect order in the middle and the names in the pupils' native language on the right. Ask pupils to match the animal with its young and then with the meaning in their native language.
Some possible English examples are: cat-kitten, cow-calf, deer-fawn, dog-puppy, duck-duckling, frog-tadpole, goat-kid, goose-gosling, hare-leveret, horse-foal, kangaroo-joey, lion-cub, pig-piglet, seal-pub, sheep-lamb, swan-cygnet.

Wordsearches

Pupils can make a wordsearch for their partners based on a particular group of words such as herbs, spring flowers, fruit, vegetables, garden flowers or animals and their young.

A game: Fruit salad/Vegetable soup/Bunch of flowers/Herd of animals

The name of the game depends on which group of words you decide to use.
Pupils sit in a circle. One pupil stands in the middle. Choose four different types of fruit (vegetable/flower/animal/etc.), for example apples, pears, peaches, plums. Designate one of the names to each pupil. (There will then be a number of pupils with the same name.) The pupil in the middle has no name. This pupil then calls out one of the names, for example "pears". Now all the "pears" must change places. The pupil in the middle must try to find a place to sit, too. The person left without a seat stands in the middle and calls another of the names, for example "apples". This time all the "apples" must change places. When the pupil in the middle calls "fruit salad" (vegetable soup/bunch of flowers/herd of animals) everyone has to change places.

8 Festivals in April and May

These copy masters cover Easter, April Fools' Day and Mothering Sunday.

Easter – Copy master 8.1 (page 76)

Easter is not celebrated in a big way in Britain. At breakfast on Easter Sunday people exchange chocolate Easter eggs and some families go to church, but little more is done on a large scale. The text on the worksheet describes Easter in America. After reading it pupils can compare Easter celebrations in their country to Easter in the USA. If there are pupils from other countries in your class encourage them to talk about Easter celebrations (if any) where they come from. Ask pupils of non-Christian religions if they celebrate anything around the time of Easter, e.g. Jewish Passover.

There is a list of words below, which pupils should be familiar with in connection with Easter. On the worksheet there is also an explanation of how to work out the date of Easter each year.

Easter vocabulary

chick – a young chicken often featured on Easter cards
daffodil – yellow flower which blooms in spring
Easter bonnet – smart hat which is worn at Easter parades
egg rolling – a game in which coloured, hard-boiled eggs are rolled down a hill
egg shackling – a game in which people bang coloured, hard-boiled eggs together
Eostre – Anglo-Saxon goddess of spring: the word Easter is derived from her name
Good Friday – the Friday before Easter Sunday
Hot cross buns – spiced buns which are marked with a cross and traditionally eaten on Good Friday in Britain
Lent – the forty days leading up to Easter.
Maundy Thursday – the Thursday before Easter. In England a ceremony is held usually in Westminster Abbey on Maundy Thursday in which the Queen gives specially minted money (so-called Maundy money) to as many men and women as her age.

Egg trouble again – Copy masters 8.2a and 8.2b (pages 77/78)

The story is recorded on the cassette. Pupils should read the text whilst listening and then answer the following questions.

1. What had been different during the Grand Congress compared to everyday life at the palace?
   Everyone at the palace had had to be on their best behaviour and had not been able to relax. The King and Queen had tried to impress their guests, for example, by wearing the real crown instead of a plastic one, by keeping everything tidy and by wearing their best clothes.
2. How do the King and Queen like their boiled eggs?
   The King likes his hard-boiled and the Queen likes hers runny.
3. Why didn't the King and Queen simply exchange eggs when they got the wrong ones each morning?
   Because they were afraid someone might notice and there would then be a scandal in the newspapers!
4. Why did they always get the wrong eggs?
   Because they were taking them from the opposite side of the tray and the Butler forgot to take this into account when he was offering the eggs to them.
5. How was the problem finally solved?
   The Lord Chamberlain told the cook to mark the eggs soft and hard before boiling them, so that the King and Queen would know which ones to take.

When pupils are familiar with the text ask them to work in groups of five and take on the roles of King, Queen, Cook, Butler, and Lord Chamberlain. They can then perform the story as a play or radio play.

Further activity – 'Egg-spressions'

Ask pupils to look up the following 'egg-spressions' in a dictionary and explain their meanings.

- to put all your eggs in one basket
- as sure as eggs is eggs
- to have egg on your face
- to count your chickens before they are hatched

April Fool's Day – Copy master 8.3 (page 79)

Use this worksheet on April 1st. Ask pupils to correct the text on the copy master. Pupils should then rewrite the text with the correct spellings. The correct version is given below. There are 50 mistakes in the text. The words underlined are spelt wrongly on the copy master. You could copy the version below onto an OHP transparency so that pupils can check that their texts are correct.

The illustrations on the copy master show some common tricks. Ask pupils to explain these and describe any tricks they have played on April Fools' Day.

About April Fools' Day

April Fools' Day is on April 1st. People all over the world play tricks on each other on this day!
No-one quite knows when April Fools' Day was first celebrated. There are different theories. But it probably dates back to ancient times when the Spring equinox marked the beginning of the New Year. April 1st may well have been the last day of a week of New Year festivities.
The idea of playing tricks on April 1st probably began in France in 1564. It was then that the French decided to change their calendar. January 1st became New Year's Day. It had previously been the custom to exchange New Year presents and messages on April 1st, and so now joke presents and messages were given on April 1st in memory of the old New Year's Day! Maybe some people even forgot that the dates had been changed and still celebrated New Year's week at the end of March. These people might have been the first April fools!
The April fool custom spread from France throughout Europe and to America. On one April Fool's Day in Britain in the 19th century lots of people gathered at the Tower of London because they had received invitations to watch 'The annual ceremony of the washing of the white lions'. This was, of course, a joke, which many people fell for! Nowadays spoof reports are published in many newspapers and broadcast on television, often making April Fools of thousands of people! One famous TV programme on April 1st reported on the spaghetti harvest in Italy. It showed workers picking spaghetti from trees!
Children and young people especially enjoy playing tricks. One typical trick, which is very easy and effective, is simply to stand somewhere public and look up or point at the sky as if you have seen something. You then just wait for other people to join in. There is however one rule about playing tricks on April Fools' Day in Britain: all jokes must be played by noon. If you play a trick on someone after twelve o'clock you are the April Fool!

Mother's Day – Copy master 8.4 (page 80)

Pupils must read the text and decide whether the statements in the table are true for Britain, America or both. The solution is given below.

Statement	True for Mothering Sunday in Britain	True for Mother's Day in the USA
1. It is a day when love and respect is shown for mothers and grandmothers.	✔	✔
2. It dates back to the 17th century.	✔	
3. It was first celebrated in May 1908.		✔
4. It is always celebrated on the second Sunday in May.		✔
5. It is always celebrated on the fourth Sunday in Lent.	✔	
6. Carnations are traditionally associated with this day.		✔
7. Simnel cakes used to be a traditional gift for mothers on this day.	✔	
8. Anna M. Jarvis started a campaign to have a special day declared in honour of all mothers.		✔
9. It used to be the only day in Lent when games could be played.	✔	
10. People working away from home were given the day off to visit their families.	✔	
11. West Virginia was the first state to adopt an official Mother's Day.		✔
12. Today it has become a rather commercialized event.	✔	(✔)

9 Summer

Use these worksheets in June or July.

Song: Summer in the city

Music/Text: John Sebastian and Steve Boone
© by Hudson Bay Music Co., USA. All rights for Germany, Austria, Switzerland and E. Europe held by EMI Music Publishing Germany GmbH

A Verse 1
Hot town, summer in the city,
Back o' my neck gettin' dirt and gritty.
Been down, isn't it a pity,
Doesn't seem to be a shadow in the city.
All around people lookin' half dead,
Walkin' on a sidewalk hotter than a match head.

B Chorus
But tonight it's a different world,
Go out and find a girl.
Come on, come on and dance all night,
Despite the heat it'll be allright and babe,
Don't you know it's a pity the days
Can't be like the nights
In the summer in the city,
In the summer in the city.

A Verse 2
Cool town, evenin' in the city,
Dressed so fine and a-lookin' so pretty.
Cool cat, lookin' for a kitty,
Gonna look in ev'ry corner of the city.
Till I'm wheezin' like a bus stop,
Runnin' up the stairs, gonna meet you at the roof top.

B Chorus

A Verse 1

B Chorus

This is the ideal song to listen to or sing on a hot summer's day.
Play the song to the pupils. Tell them to listen carefully and decide what they think the title of the song might be, and to find out what time of day it is when the singer is singing. (*Solution:* evening/night) Then explain any new vocabulary to your class, and play the song again. Pupils should then answer the following questions.

Verse 1

1. How does the singer describe a) the city; b) the people and c) himself in the first verse?
   a) hot, no shadows; b) they look half dead; c) his neck is hot and dirty
2. Is he singing about daytime or night-time in the first verse? *daytime*

Chorus

3. What does the singer plan to do that evening?
   He's going to go out and find a girlfriend and go dancing.
4. Why do you think he would like the days to be like the nights?
   Because the nights are cooler and at night he can go looking for a girl.

Verse 2

5. How does the singer describe a) himself and b) the city in this verse?
   a) He's dressed in nice clothes and looking good. He feels 'cool'!
   b) He describes it as cool.
6. Who is he referring to as 'cat' and 'kitty'?
   He is the 'cat' and the girl he is looking for is the 'kitty'.
7. Write a poem describing a hot summer's day or evening in the place where you live.

A change in the Earth's climate – Copy master 9.1 (page 81)

June 5th is World Environment Day, a good opportunity to talk about environmental problems throughout the world in class. This worksheet can be used in bi-lingual classes learning geography in English. It provides information about the danger of the Earth's climate changing as a result of the greenhouse effect, acid rain, and the ozone hole. Read the texts with the pupils and then ask them to complete the table below, which you can copy onto an OHP transparency. Keep the answers covered until pupils have completed the task. Tell them to copy the table into their exercise books.

Causes of change to the climate	What is this?	What causes this to happen?	What can/will happen as a result of this?	What can be done to avoid it?
The greenhouse effect	*A layer of gas is building up in the atmosphere around the earth. The gas acts like the glass on a greenhouse: it let's heat in, but not out.*	*Gases like carbon dioxide are formed when fuels such as wood, coal, oil, gas and petrol are burnt. These gases are now building up in the atmosphere around the Earth.*	*The temperature of the Earth will increase. This is known as global warming. This increase in temperature will cause the ice in the polar regions to melt, which will cause floods and so also ultimately lead to hunger and diseases.*	*People can stop burning so much fuel at home and for industrial purposes. For example, people could stop using their cars so often. We should make better use of other energy sources such as solar power, wind power and water power.*
Acid rain	*This is rain which has been polluted by chemicals released from factory chimneys, power stations and vehicle exhausts.*	*Factories, power stations and vehicles release poisonous chemicals into the air. These rise up and react with substances in the atmosphere to create mild acids. The acid then falls back down to the Earth in the rain.*	*Trees and plants are killed by the rain. Fish and other creatures in our waters are poisoned, stonework on buildings and statues is damaged.*	*We must stop polluting the air with exhaust fumes and stop burning so much fuel in factories and power stations.*
The ozone hole	*The ozone layer surrounds the Earth and filters out many of the sun's harmful rays. The ozone hole is where the ozone layer has become very thin – especially over the South pole – and now lets the harmful rays in.*	*The chemicals in some aerosol sprays and the cooling fluid in some refridgerators damage the ozone layer.*	*More and more harmful rays from the sun can get to the Earth causing an increase in skin cancer.*	*We should avoid buying and using sprays and other goods which contain the harmful chemicals.*

London Trip – Copy masters 9.2a and 9.2b (pages 82/83)

Pupils in England often go on school outings in the summer term, when the weather is often good and the end of the school year is not far away. London is still a popular choice for a day out. On copy master 9.2a there is a humourous poem about a school trip to London. Copy master 9.2b is a simplified map of London which features the items mentioned in the poem. This poem could be read at any time of the year when London is being dealt with in class. You could copy the map onto a transparency and present it via the OHP.

Read the poem to the pupils and ask them to try to find the places mentioned on the map of London. Further information about the places mentioned is given below.

Ask pupils to change the poem into a narrative text in which they describe the trip from the point of view of a) a different pupil; b) the teacher; c) the bus driver.

Pupils could also act out different scenes from the poem.

Further information: In London

(The following museums and sights are all mentioned in the poem 'London Trip'.)

The Tower of London: William the Conqueror began building the Tower in 1078 as a castle and palace. Since then it has been used as a fortress, a zoo, a Royal court, a prison and place of execution. Many people including Elizabeth I, Sir Walter Raleigh and Anne Boleyn were held prisoner in the Tower for their religious beliefs or suspected treason. During World Wars I and II spies were held prisoner there. Today at the Tower of London you can see the Crown Jewels as well as the armoury, which is full of suits of armour and a display of torture instruments!

The Victoria and Albert Museum (V & A) has Britain's largest collection of tapestries, costumes, jewellery and glassware. It also has a collection of paintings by many famous artists. In the costume gallery you can see clothes from the past to the present day: from the 1540s to designer clothes from the end of the twentieth century.

The Zoo is in Regent's Park. It was opened in 1827. Today there are more than 8,000 animals in the zoo, some of which are very rare. You can adopt an animal at London Zoo for a year: the cost depends on the animal you choose and how much it eats!

The changing of the guard at Buckingham Palace (The Palace Guards): Buckingham Palace is the official home of the Queen. Nowadays it is possible to visit certain parts of the Palace at certain times of the year. The changing of the guard takes place every day in summer or every other day in winter. It is said to be the best free show in London!

Trafalgar Square was named to commemorate Admiral Lord Nelson's victory over the French at the Battle of Trafalgar in 1805. The Square's most famous landmark is Nelson's Column, which is 51 metres high and has a 5 metre high statue of Nelson on the top of it. There are four huge bronze lions at the bottom of the Column. There are thousands of pigeons in Trafalgar Square and you can buy birdseed there and let them eat it out of your hand.

St Paul's Cathedral was designed by Sir Christopher Wren after the Great Fire of London destroyed the original cathedral in 1666. You can walk up the 666 steps to the famous dome, which is 111 metres high, and visit the Whispering Gallery: if you whisper towards the wall on one side of the dome you can be heard clearly on the other side!

The Science Museum is full of displays and exhibitions designed to help people understand science and technology from the past and present. There are machines and there is special technology including real spacecraft. There is also a special section in the museum about the history of medicine.

The Royal Albert Hall is a famous concert hall. It was built in 1867-1871. It is built in the shape of a huge oval amphitheatre and has space for up to 6,000 people.

The Tate Gallery contains the nation's most important collection of contemporary art as well as British art from Elizabethan times including work by William Gainsborough, William Blake and Francis Bacon.

The Blackwall Tunnel is actually two tunnels under the River Thames for vehicles – one for vehicles travelling south and the other for northbound traffic. It is situated to the east of the Isle of Dogs. Before the M25 London Orbital Motorway was completed these tunnels were used by almost all traffic travelling to SE England from north of London and vice versa. There were often traffic jams and long delays there.

Further activity

Ask pupils to try to find brochures, guidebooks, photos or even videos about London and to collect information about the sights mentioned in the text. They could then make a London scrapbook in which they write the poem out and illustrate it with photos, etc.

Typically British

Pupils should listen to the information given below (it is recorded on the cassette) about the two famous summer events in Britain. They should then answer the questions below, which you can copy and hand out to them. Check that their answers are correct before telling them to use their solutions and write their own texts about the two events. You could ask pupils to find photos in magazines, brochures etc. to illustrate their work. Both events are generally broadcast internationally on television and you could try to make a video recording to show to pupils.

The Trooping of the Colour

Queen Elizabeth II's real birthday is on 21st April, but her official birthday is celebrated on the second Saturday in June.
On the Queen's official birthday there is a traditional ceremony called the "Trooping of the Colour". This is a big military parade with bands and hundreds of soldiers, many of them on horseback, which takes place at Horse Guards' Parade, in London's Whitehall. The Queen always attends this ceremony wearing the uniform of the regiment whose colour (flag) is being trooped (shown to the troops). The Queen arrives on horseback (riding side-saddle) and during the ceremony the guardsmen march and ride past her with enormous precision displaying their flags. Thousands of people and tourists watch the colourful ceremony at Whitehall and millions watch it on TV throughout the world. After the ceremony the Queen and her family return to Buckingham Palace and appear on its famous balcony to wave to the crowds.

The Wimbledon Lawn Tennis Championships

This is probably the most famous tennis tournament in the world and takes place at the end of June and the beginning of July every year. Lawn tennis was first introduced to Wimbledon in 1875 and in 1877 the first championships were held there. At first most of the players came from England but soon players from abroad also came to compete and in 1905 May Sutton, an American, became the first overseas champion. The present Wimbledon site in Church Road, Wimbledon was opened by King George V in 1922. Apart from during World War II the world's leading tennis tournament has taken place there every summer since then. In the two Wimbledon weeks people young and old stand for hours in mile long queues hoping to get day tickets and the chance to see their favourite tennis stars. But it is not only the chance to see the world's top tennis players which attracts such huge crowds, it is the whole Wimbledon atmosphere: the strawberries and cream, the rather small and old-fashioned looking tennis courts and buildings – by comparison to other major tennis stadiums in the world. People say what makes Wimbledon so popular with the spectators and the players is quite simply 'Wimbledon magic'!

Questions

The Trooping of the Colour

1. When is Queen Elizabeth II's real birthday?
2. When does the Trooping of the Colour take place and what does it celebrate?
3. What kind of parade is the Trooping of the Colour?
4. Where does it take place?
5. What does the Queen wear to the ceremony?
6. What does the Trooping of the Colour mean?
7. How does the Queen arrive at the ceremony?
8. Who can watch the ceremony?
9. What do the Queen and her family do after the ceremony?

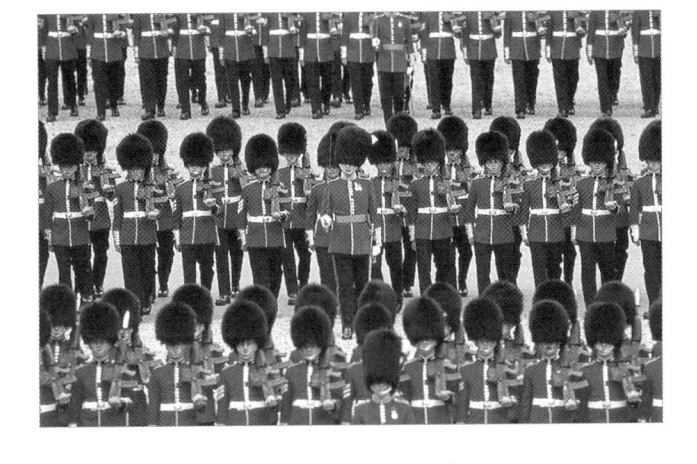

The Wimbledon Lawn Tennis Championships

1. When is 'Wimbledon' each year?
2. When was Lawn tennis first introduced to Wimbledon?
3. What took place in 1877?
4. Where did most of the players come from at first?
5. Who was May Sutton?
6. Where is the present Wimbledon site?
7. Who was it opened by and when?
8. When were the championships not held?
9. What must people do if they want to get day tickets?
10. According to the text, why do so many people go to Wimbledon?

Solution to questions

The Trooping of the Colour

1. *21st April*
2. *the second Saturday in June/the Queen's official birthday*
3. *a big military parade with bands and hundreds of soldiers*
4. *at Horse Guards' Parade, Whitehall, London*
5. *the uniform of the regiment that is trooping the colour*
6. *the colour is the flag of the regiment/trooping means showing to the troops (soldiers)*
7. *on horseback, side-saddle*
8. *everyone - live at Whitehall or on TV throughout the world*
9. *they go back to Buckingham Palace and wave to the crowds from the balcony*

Wimbledon

1. *end of June/beginning of July*
2. *in 1875*
3. *the first championships were held*
4. *from England*
5. *the first foreign champion: she came from America and won Wimbledon in 1905*
6. *in Church Road, Wimbledon*
7. *by King George V in 1922*
8. *during World War II*
9. *stand for hours in mile long queues*
10. *to see the world's top tennis players, to eat strawberries and cream, to see the stadium, to experience the Wimbledon atmosphere/Wimbledon magic*

Further activity

The Trooping of the Colour and Wimbledon are only two of many events which take place in Britain every summer. Ask your pupils to write to the British Tourist Association either in their country or in Britain and ask for further information about any of the events listed below.

The Epsom Derby: a famous horse-race held in early June at the Epsom Racecourse.

Royal Ascot: horseracing held in late June at the Royal Ascot racecourse, famous for its parade of fashion and in particular hats on 'Ladies Day'.

The Lords Test Match: This is an international cricket match in which the England cricket team plays at the Lords Cricket Ground in the presence of the Queen.

Henley Regatta: rowing races (and more) held on the River Thames at Henley at the end of June/beginning of July.

The Proms: a series of classical concerts in the Royal Albert Hall held over two months in the summer.

The Edinburgh Festival: Europe's biggest Art Festival with artists and performances from all over the world held in Edinburgh in August.

✱ All American: Fourth of July and Flag Day – Copy master 9.3 (page 84)

Information about these two American holidays is given on the worksheet in the form of a cloze text. The text is recorded on the cassette. Pupils have to fill in the words underlined whilst or after listening to the text.

Solution

Only five national holiday days in the USA today are celebrated in all of the states. These are Labor Day (the first Monday in September), Thanksgiving Day (the fourth Thursday in November), Christmas Day, New Year's Day, and *Independence Day* (the 4th July).

Independence Day is one of the most *important* holidays in the USA. It commemorates the day when the United States declared its *independence* from Britain – on the 4th July, 1776. The Declaration of Independence was *signed* in Independence Hall, Pennsylvania, and this document marks the beginning of the *history* of the United States of America.

On 4th July flags and decorations are _put out_ in the streets and on public buildings. Every village, town and city has _parades_, games or rodeos. Some people have picnics and _barbecues_, others go on trips to the beach or to the _country_, and in the evening there are magnificent firework displays to celebrate America's birthday.

Flag Day is celebrated on 14th June. It commemorates the day in 1777 when the Stars and Stripes became the official flag of the USA. The flag has thirteen alternate _stripes_ of _red_ and _white_, which represent the thirteen _colonies_ that became independent from Britain in 1776. The white stars on the _blue_ background indicate the number of _states_ in the union. As each new state was adopted, another star was _added_ to the original thirteen, and there are now 50 altogether. The last two _states_ to join the Union were Alaska, in 1959, and Hawaii, in 1960. On Flag Day the Stars and Stripes is displayed in front of most public and many private _buildings_. Flag Day is not a public holiday in the USA, so banks, schools, offices and businesses stay _open_.

✳ Further activity

Ask pupils to draw the Stars and Stripes on a large piece of paper. They can then write the names of the thirteen colonies on the thirteen alternate stripes of red and white. (The original colonies were: Massachusetts, New Hampshire, New York, Rhode Island, Connecticut, New Jersey, Delaware, Pennsylvania, Maryland, Virginia, North Carolina, South Carolina and Georgia.) They can find out the names of the current states in an atlas or on a map of America and write these around the outside of the flag. They could also use an encyclopaedia to find out when each of the states joined the union. Below is an alphabetical list of all the current states of America giving the date when each state joined the Union and each state's rank of joining.

Alabama: 14.12.1819 (22nd)
Alaska: 3.1.1959 (49th)
Arizona: 14.2.1912 (48th)
Arkansas: 15.6.1836 (25th)
California: 9.9.1850 (31st)
Colorado: 1.8.1876 (38th)
Connecticut: 9.1.1788 (5th)
Delaware: 7.12.1787 (1st)
District of Columbia: 3.3.1845 (27th)
Georgia: 2.1.1788 (4th)
Hawaii: 21.8.1959 (50th)
Idaho: 3.7.1890 (43rd)
Illinois: 3.12.1818 (21st)
Indiana: 11.12.1816 (19th)
Iowa: 28.12.1846 (29th)
Kansas: 29.1.1861 (34th)
Kentucky: 1.6.1792 (15th)

Louisiana: 30.4.1812 (18th)
Maine: 15.3.1820 (23rd)
Maryland: 28.4.1788 (7th)
Massachusetts: 6.2.1788 (6th)
Michigan: 26.1.1837 (26th)
Minnesota: 11.2.1858 (32nd)
Mississippi: 10.12.1817 (20th)
Missouri: 10.8.1821 (24th)
Montana: 8.11.1889 (41st)
Nebraska: 1.3.1867 (37th)
New Hampshire: 21.6.1788 (9th)
New Jersey: 18.12.1787 (3rd)
New Mexico: 6.1.1912 (47th)
New York: 26.7.1788 (11th)
Nevada: 31.10.1864 (36th)
North Carolina: 21.11.1789 (12th)
North Dakota: 2.11.1889 (39th)

Ohio: 1.3.1803 (17th)
Oklahoma: 16.11.1907 (46th)
Oregon: 14.2.1859 (33rd)
Pennsylvania: 12.12.1787 (2nd)
Rhode Island: 29.5.1790 (13th)
South Carolina: 23.5.1788 (8th)
South Dakota: 2.11.1889 (40th)
Tennessee: 1.6.1796 (16th)
Texas: 29.12.1845 (28th)
Utah: 4.1.1896 (45th)
Vermont: 4.3.1791 (14th)
Virginia: 25.6.1788 (10th)
Washington: 11.11.1889 (42nd)
West Virginia: 20.6.1863 (35th)
Wisconsin: 29.5.1848 (30th)
Wyoming: 10.7.1890 (44th)

American English (AE) – British English (BE) – Copy master 9.4 (page 85)

Instructions for playing this 'pairs' game are given on the worksheet. Pupils can play in pairs or groups of three or four. Pupils can add more AE-BE equivalents of their own to make the game more difficult.

Solution

apartment–flat; backpack–rucksack; bill–note; cookie–biscuit; diaper–nappy; elevator–lift; fall–autumn; first floor–ground floor; gas–petrol; hood–bonnet; intersection–crossroads; movies–cinema; pacifier–dummy; parking lot–car park; railroad–railway; rest-room–toilet; sidewalk–pavement; subway–underground; trailer–caravan; trunk–boot; truck–lorry; undershirt–vest; vacation–holiday(s); washbag–toilet bag; yield sign–give way sign

10 School's out!

This chapter brings the school year to an end. It includes songs to sing or listen to, poems to read, recite or learn by heart and games to play.

Song: Summer holiday

Music/Text: Bruce Welch and Brian Bennett
© 1963 & 1987 EMI Music Publishing Ltd,
trading as Elstree Music, London WC2H 0LD

[A] Verse 1
We're all going on a summer holiday,
No more working for a week or two,
Fun and laughter on a summer holiday,
No more worries for me or you
For a week or two.

[B] Chorus
We're going where the sun shines brightly,
We're going where the sea is blue,
We've seen it in the movies,
Now let's see if it's true.

[A] Verse 2
Everybody has a summer holiday,
Doing things they always wanted to,
So we're going on a summer holiday,
To make our dreams come true,
For me and you.

[B] Chorus

[A] Verse 3
Everybody has a summer holiday,
Doing things they always wanted to,
So we're going on a summer holiday,
To make our dreams come true,
For me and you.

Play the song to the pupils and ask them to try to work out the text of the song. You could write a rough framework of the song on the board giving one word or phrase from each line of the song. The suggestion below is for the first verse:
1. We're..,
   ....working................................. ,
   ....laughter..,
   ....worries..,
   ....or two.

You will best be able to decide how many words or phrases your group will need to help them work out the text. More able groups might well be able to carry out the task without being given any help at all.
The song has an easy melody! Ask your class to sing it!
The song expresses very positive feelings towards summer holidays. After working with the song you could give pupils copy master 10.1 and look at the poem 'Last Day of the Summer Term'. You could then discuss the differences in atmosphere created by the song and the poem and ask pupils to explain which of the two they prefer and why. (See also below, copy master 10.1.)

Last day – at last! – Copy master 10.1 (page 86)

There are two poems and a reproduction of a subject report for a pupil at an English school on the copy master.

Last Day of the Summer Term

This poem makes a good contrast to the song *Summer Holiday*, which clearly expresses very happy feelings about summer holidays. The poem looks at the summer holidays from the point of view of someone who is not going away and is not looking forward to the holidays. Use the poem on its own or in contrast to the song. You can also use the poem to introduce a discussion about the fact that there are people who – for different reasons – cannot go on holiday.

- Read the poem to the pupils first, then ask them to read it to each other in groups paying attention to the atmosphere of the poem.
- Ask pupils to describe the holiday plans which the different children in the poem have.
- Some popular British holiday resorts and areas are mentioned in the poem: Brighton, the Norfolk Broads and the Isle of Wight. Pupils could look up these places on a map of Britain and find out what the typical features of the landscape in these places are.
- They can then talk about the type of things people might do when they are on holiday in these places and discuss which places they would most/least like to visit.
- Ask pupils why they think Jane, the speaker in the poem, does not go on holiday. (Pupils might come up with the following answers: *She probably lives alone with her mother. Her father may be dead. Her parents might be divorced. Her mother might not have enough money to go on holiday.*)
- Pupils can talk about their own holiday plans. They can make lists of activities, places to go and things to do at home and on holiday. They could make a brochure about what young people can do in their area in the summer.
- Pupils could do a class survey to find out where pupils are going and what they plan to do during the long summer holidays.

Bad Reports – Good Manners

In many countries including Britain pupils get their school reports on the last day of the summer term. Spike Milligan's poem is a comical look at the way a father reacts to his son's bad report and the son's excuse for his poor achievement.

- After reading the poem ask pupils if there is any difference between the kind of information given on this British school report and the reports they get. (The report states that the boy was bottom of the class. It is still common in some – nowadays mostly private/public – schools to put the pupil's position in the class in each subject and in the class as a whole on the pupil's report.)
- Ask pupils to explain the ambiguity of the last two lines: When would standing aside have been the right thing to do?
- Ask pupils how their parents react to the grades, etc. on their reports: Do they get told off if they get bad marks? Do they get rewarded (and how) if they get good marks?

School subject report

After dealing with the poem look at the reproduction of a subject report for German which appears at the bottom of the worksheet. This is a typical report form from a modern British comprehensive school. It is for a Year 9 pupil. Apart from an evaluation of skills and effort it also includes the results of the German exam.

- Ask pupils to look at the report form and answer the following questions:
  1. Which aspects of German is Laura best at?
  2. Which are her weaker skills?
  3. How does Laura behave in German lessons according to her report?
  4. What do you understand by effort and attitude?
  5. Which is the highest and which is the lowest grade a pupil can get?
  6. Does Laura's achievement relate to her class or set? Or to the year as a whole?
- Then give pupils any of the additional information on page 44 about school reports which they are not already familiar with.

Ask pupils to compare the reports they get with British school reports: When do pupils get their reports? How many times a year do they get reports? What are their reports like? Are there only grades on their reports or is any other information given about the progress a pupil has made?

- Discuss the advantages and disadvantages of the different systems and discuss which type of reports pupils would prefer.
- Finally you could ask pupils to assess themselves for English according to the criteria on the report form on the worksheet. They should write a comment on themselves in the comment space. If you have time, you could do the same for each pupil in your class, so that they could compare your view of them with their own.

> **School reports in Britain**
>
> In Britain, pupils get their school reports at the end of the summer term. The reports are usually in form of small booklets. There is usually a report from the tutor or form teacher about the pupil's overall achievement and behaviour in the class, this generally concentrates on personal and social skills. Then there are individual reports from each subject teacher. The teachers often give a detailed written comment on the pupil. There is usually one page for each subject. In the first years of secondary school it is also now very common for pupils to write a report on themselves. They write down whether – in their opinion – they have made any progress or what their problems were. They can say if they enjoyed a subject or found it quite difficult. Teachers can comment on the pupils' reports from their point of view. As well as having a series of tests throughout the year in secondary schools there are end of year exams in most subjects. The results of these exams are usually given on the report form and determine to a large extent the grade the pupil gets.

❋ European countries and their capitals – Copy master 10.2 (page 87)

Pupils must list as many of the European countries and capitals shown on the map as they can (in English, of course!).
Then they can make a wordsearch for their partners. Make sure that they either use all capital or all small letters. Alternatively you could make a wordsearch for your pupils before you give them the worksheet. Ask pupils to find the names, circle them and write them down on the list on the worksheet.

Further activities

1. Wordsearches:

Make wordsearches based on other summer topics.
For example:

On the beach: ball – binoculars – boat – bucket – deck chair – flippers – lighthouse – net – pebbles – sand – sandcastle – seagull – seaweed – shell – snorkel – spade – suncream – sunglasses – swimsuit – towel – wave – yacht

Sea creatures: catfish – crab – dolphin – jellyfish – lobster – mussel – octopus – oyster – penguin – sea-elephant – sea-horse – sea urchin – seal – shark – starfish – turtle – walrus – whale

On the farm: barn – bird – bull – calf – cat – cow – chick – dog – duck – farm – farmer – fence – field – gate – hay – hedge – hen – horse – lamb – orchard – pond – sheep – stable – tractor

2. Wordsearch team game:

You will need two or three instruments like a gong, a tambourine and a bell. Make a wordsearch on one of the above topics and copy it onto a transparency. Present it to the pupils on the OHP.

1. Divide the class into two or three teams.
2. Give one instrument to each team.
3. Give each team a different coloured textmarker.
4. Call out one of the words in the wordsearch.
5. Each team must try to find the word in the wordsearch. When they have found it they make a sound with their instrument.
6. The first team to make a sound with their instrument can mark the word in the puzzle.

The team which finds the most words is the winner.

❋ The Round Europe Race – Copy masters 10.3a and 10.3b (pages 88/89)

This is a board game. It can be played by two to four players. Each player needs a counter. Each group of players needs one game board (copy master 10.3a), one set of question/answer cards (copy master 10.3b) and a dice. Brief instructions for how to play the game are given on copy master 10.3b. It is advisable to stick the game board and the cards onto sheets of card before using them. <u>The question and answer cards need to be cut out and then the number of the question/answer must be written on the back preceded by either Q (for question) or A (for answer).</u> Pupils place the question cards face down (so that they can only see the numbers) in a pile on the appropriate space on the game board. The answer cards are spread out face down on the table. If a player lands on a square with a question mark on it, he/she must take the first question card from the pile and answer the question. The other players check that the answer given is correct by looking at the card with the same number as the question on it. The answer card is then placed face down on the table again and the question card is placed at the bottom of the pile.

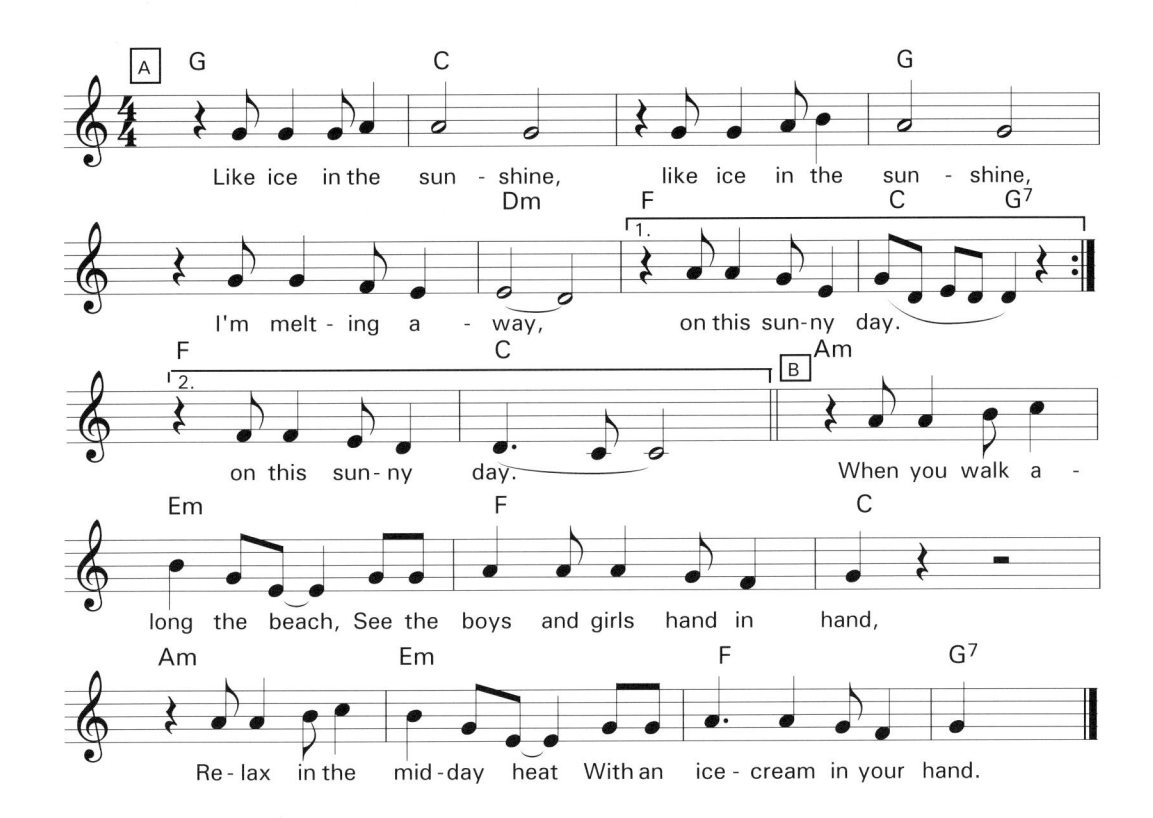

Song: Ice in the sunshine

Music/Text: Holger Julian Kopp and Hanno Harders
© 1980 by Rossl Musikverlag GmbH, Hamburg

A Chorus
Like ice in the sunshine, like ice in the sunshine,
I'm melting away, on this sunny day.

B Verse 1
When you walk along the beach,
See the boys and girls hand in hand,
Relax in the midday heat
With an ice-cream in your hand.

A Chorus

B Verse 2
If you wanna have some fun
Feeling groovy down by the sea,
Lay down in the summer sun,
Feel the good vibrations with me.

A Chorus

B Verse 3
When you're in the ocean bay
See the surfers glide out of reach,
Have fun on a sunny day
With an ice-cream on the beach.

A Chorus

Pupils may well recognise this song because it has become famous throughout the world in an advertisement for ice-cream. It is a great song to sing along to. You could ask pupils to draw or collect pictures to illustrate the song and even award a prize for the best picture(s). You may want to set pupils the following comprehension questions:

1. How does the singer say he feels? *Like ice in the sunshine, melting away*
2. Where is the singer of the song? *(Walking along) on the beach*
3. What time of day is it (in the first verse)? *Midday*
4. Who does the singer see on the beach? *Boys and girls holding hands*
5. What is the singer doing in the first verse? *Eating ice-cream and relaxing*
6. What is fun, according to the singer, in the second verse? *Lying in the sun, listening to music/the sounds around him.*
7. Who can the singer see in the third verse? *Surfers surfing away from the beach*
8. What is the difference (if any) between ice and ice-cream? *Ice is frozen water, ice-cream is a frozen cream mixture which people often eat in summer.*

45

Games for the end of term

1. The dining car

This is a rhythmical call and response game based on the (fictitious) menu of a train dining car. The menu is chanted rhythmically.

- First ask pupils to make suggestions of what you might find on a menu in a train. The suggestions should have two to four syllables. (Alternatively simply follow the example given below.)
- You call out the items on the menu, always emphasizing the first syllable, and the pupils chant each item three times after you.
- You start off very slowly and speed up as the imaginary train gathers speed. The chant finishes with a whistling: "toot-toot".

(The words/syllables printed in bold type should be emphasised.)

Teacher	**Class**
Chips and sausage,	chips and sausage, chips and sausage, chips and sausage
Bread and butter,	bread and butter, bread and butter, bread and butter
Fish and chips,	fish and chips, fish and chips, fish and chips
Egg and bacon,	egg and bacon, egg and bacon, egg and bacon
Ploughman's lunch,	ploughman's lunch, ploughman's lunch
Fruit salad,	fruit salad, fruit salad, fruit salad
Apple pie,	apple pie, apple pie, apple pie
Ice-cream,	ice-cream, ice-cream, ice-cream
Tea and milk,	tea and milk, tea and milk, tea and milk
Toot-toot,	toot-toot, toot-toot, toot-toot.

2. I'm going to London

The object of the game is to 'buy' three things beginning with the same letter as the first letter of the town given. A new town must always start with a different letter to the previous one. The same objects should not be repeated at a later stage in the game. Before starting decide whether to use English/American towns only or to allow pupils to use the names of towns in their own country as well.

- Make two teams, A and B.
- Team A begins by saying "You're going to *London* to buy:"
- Team B must now complete the sentence by naming three objects they might buy there beginning with 'L', for example: lamps, lettuce, lobsters.
- If team B can name three things within twenty seconds they get a point and continue: "You're going to *Brighton* to buy:"
- Now Team A must name three objects beginning with 'B' and so on.
- If the objects cannot be named within the time limit the other team gets the point and can start the sentence again choosing a different town. If a team can't think of the name of a town the other team gets a point and can start the sentence.

The first team to get 10 points is the winner.

SCHOOL IS COOL!
– POEMS AND RHYMES ABOUT SCHOOL

God made bees

God made bees
Bees make honey
We do the work
But teachers get the money!

(Anon)

Writing Right

Said a boy to his teacher one day
"Wright has not written 'rite' right, I say!"
And the teacher replied
As the error she eyed:
"Right! – Wright, write 'rite' right, right away!"

(Anon)

Latin

Latin is a language
As dead as dead can be,
First it killed the Romans
And now it's killing me.

(Anon)

CHESTER

Chester come to school and said,
"Durn, I growed another head."
Teacher said, "It's time you knowed
The word is 'grew' instead of 'growed'."

(Shel Silverstein)

School Dinners

If you stay to school dinners
Better throw them aside.
A lot of kids didn't,
A lot of kids died.
The meat is of iron,
The puds are of steel.
If the gravy don't get you,
The custard will.

(trad.)

Punctuation Puzzle

Caesar entered on his head
A helmet on each foot
A sandal in his hands he had
His trusty sword to boot.

(Anon)

It's School Today

I wake up early, it's school today.
I'll get up early and be on my way.
I wash my face, I brush my hair,
I hang my nightdress on the chair.
The breakfast table is all set,
I'll eat it quickly and feed my pet,
I wave to mum and shut the gate;
I'll have to hurry, it's half past eight.
The bus has gone. I'll run to school.
I pass the shops and the swimming pool
I reach the gate: it's five past nine,
Goodness me! I'm just in time.

(Anon)

I love to do my homework

I love do to my homework.
It makes me feel so good.
I love to do exactly
As my teachers say I should.

I love do to my homework,
I never miss a day.
I even love the men in white
Who are taking me away.

(Anon)

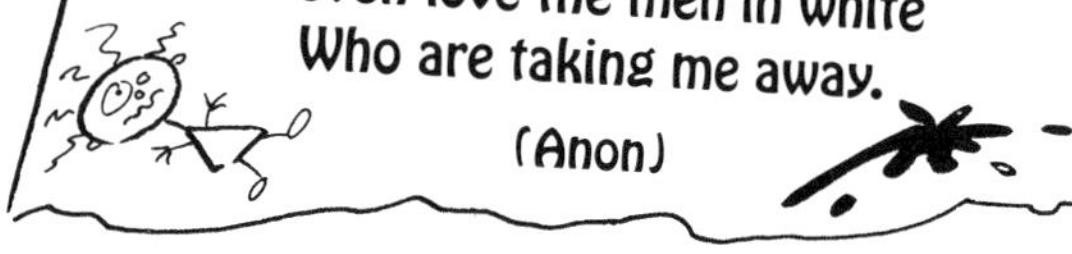

Two poems for the first day of school

How do you feel the day before a new school year begins?
Work with a partner and make a list of adjectives. Then try to say why you feel that way.

LOOK OUT!

The witches mumble horrid chants,
You're scolded by five thousand aunts,
A Martian pulls a fearsome face
And hurls you into Outer Space,
You're tied in front of whistling trains,
A tomahawk has sliced your brains,
The tigers snarl, the giants roar,
You're sat on by a dinosaur.
In vain you're shouting "Help" and "Stop",
The walls are spinning like a top,
The earth is melting in the sun
And all the horror's just begun.
And, oh, the screams, the thumping hearts –
That awful night before school starts.

(Max Fatchen)

How does the author feel about the start of school?

Make a list of things which are typical of holiday time and of term time. Add any ideas from the poem.
What do you think Russell Hoban feels about school?

SUMMER GOES
(Russel Hoban)

Summer goes, summer goes
Like the sand between my toes
When the waves go out.
That's how summer pulls away,
Leaves me standing here today,
Waiting for the school bus.

Summer brought, summer brought
All the frogs that I have caught,
Frogging at the pond,
Hot dogs, flowers, shells and rocks,
Postcards in my postcard box –
Places far away.

Summer took, summer took
All the lessons in my book,
Blew them far away.
I forgot the things I knew –
Arithmetic and spelling too,
Never thought about them.

Summer's gone, summer's gone –
Fall and winter coming on,
Frosty in the morning.
Here's the school bus right on time.
I'm not really sad that I'm
Going back to school.

Which of the two poems on this page do you prefer? Give reasons.

THE GREAT SCHOOL RACE

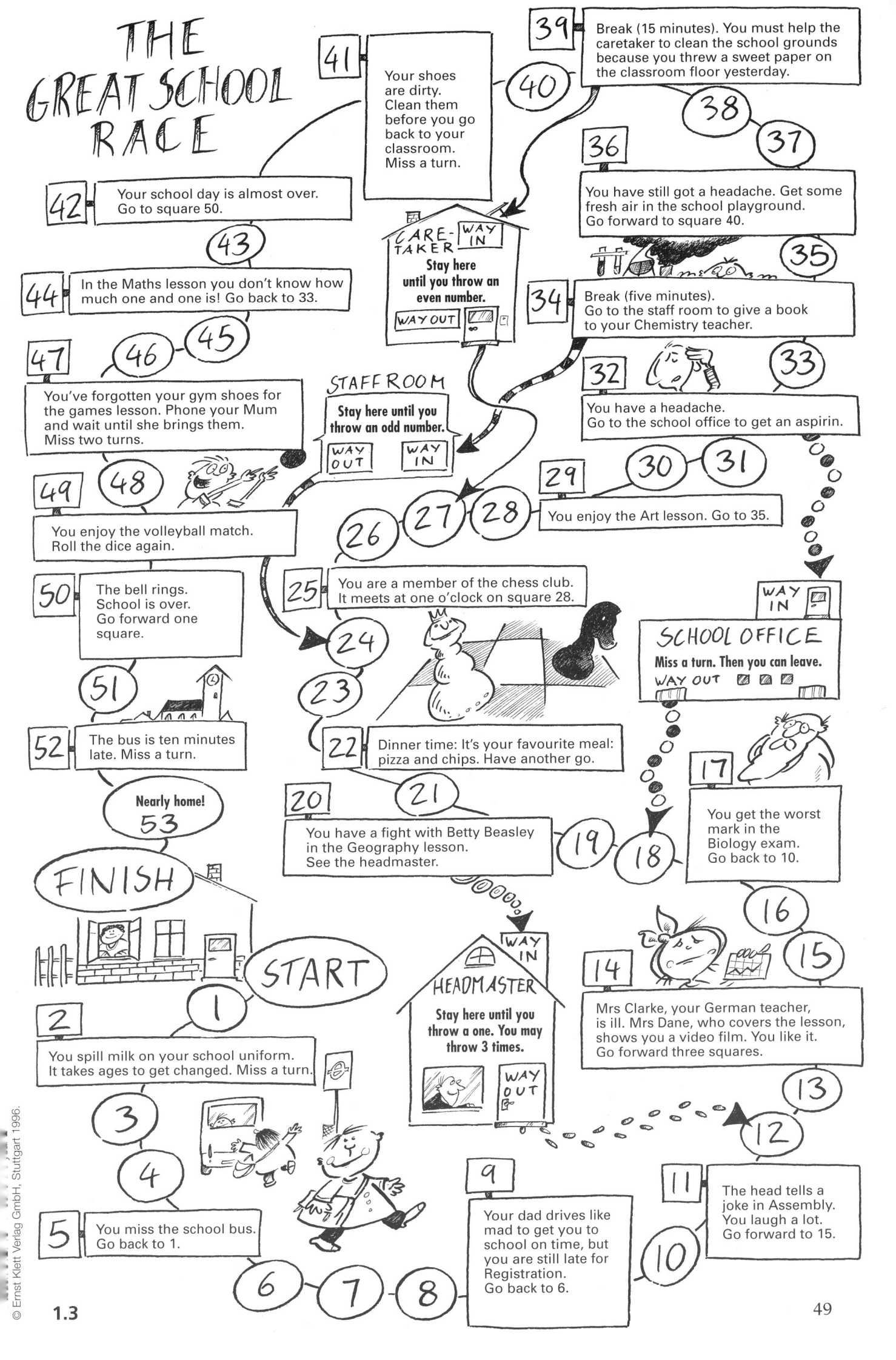

41 Your shoes are dirty. Clean them before you go back to your classroom. Miss a turn.

39 Break (15 minutes). You must help the caretaker to clean the school grounds because you threw a sweet paper on the classroom floor yesterday.

42 Your school day is almost over. Go to square 50.

36 You have still got a headache. Get some fresh air in the school playground. Go forward to square 40.

CARETAKER — Stay here until you throw an even number. WAY IN / WAY OUT

44 In the Maths lesson you don't know how much one and one is! Go back to 33.

34 Break (five minutes). Go to the staff room to give a book to your Chemistry teacher.

STAFF ROOM — Stay here until you throw an odd number. WAY OUT / WAY IN

47 You've forgotten your gym shoes for the games lesson. Phone your Mum and wait until she brings them. Miss two turns.

32 You have a headache. Go to the school office to get an aspirin.

29 You enjoy the Art lesson. Go to 35.

49 You enjoy the volleyball match. Roll the dice again.

25 You are a member of the chess club. It meets at one o'clock on square 28.

50 The bell rings. School is over. Go forward one square.

SCHOOL OFFICE — Miss a turn. Then you can leave. WAY IN / WAY OUT

22 Dinner time: It's your favourite meal: pizza and chips. Have another go.

52 The bus is ten minutes late. Miss a turn.

17 You get the worst mark in the Biology exam. Go back to 10.

Nearly home! 53

20 You have a fight with Betty Beasley in the Geography lesson. See the headmaster.

FINISH

HEADMASTER — Stay here until you throw a one. You may throw 3 times. WAY IN / WAY OUT

14 Mrs Clarke, your German teacher, is ill. Mrs Dane, who covers the lesson, shows you a video film. You like it. Go forward three squares.

START

2 You spill milk on your school uniform. It takes ages to get changed. Miss a turn.

11 The head tells a joke in Assembly. You laugh a lot. Go forward to 15.

9 Your dad drives like mad to get you to school on time, but you are still late for Registration. Go back to 6.

5 You miss the school bus. Go back to 1.

Staying home from school

Monday morning found Tom Sawyer miserable. Monday morning always found him so – because it began another week's slow suffering in school. (…)

Tom lay thinking. Presently it occurred to him that he wished he was sick: then he could stay home from school. Here was a vague possibility. He canvassed his system. No ailment was found, and he investigated again. (…)

Suddenly he discovered something. One of his upper front teeth was loose. This was lucky; he was about to begin to groan, as a "starter," as he called it, when it occurred to him that if he came into court with that argument, his aunt would pull it out, and that would hurt. So he thought he would hold the tooth in reserve for the present, and seek further. Nothing offered for some little time, and then he remembered hearing the doctor tell about a certain thing that laid up a patient for two or three weeks and threatened to make him lose a finger. So the boy eagerly drew his sore toe from under the sheet and held it up for inspection. But now he did not know the necessary symptoms. However, it seemed well worth while to chance it, so he fell to groaning with considerable spirit.

But Sid slept on unconscious.

Tom groaned louder, and fancied that he began to feel pain in the toe.

No result from Sid. (…)

Tom was aggravated. He said, "Sid, Sid!" and shook him. This course worked well, and Tom began to groan again. Sid yawned, stretched, and brought himself up on his elbow with a snort, and began to stare at Tom. Tom went on groaning. Sid said:

"Tom! Say, Tom!" [No response.] "Here, Tom! Tom! What is the matter, Tom?" And he shook him and looked in his face anxiously.

Tom moaned out:

"Oh, don't, Sid. Don't joggle me."

"Why, what's the matter, Tom? I must call auntie."

"No – never mind. It'll be over by and by, maybe. Don't call anybody."

"But I must! Don't groan so, Tom, it's awful. How long you been this way?"

"Hours. Ouch! Oh, don't stir so, Sid, you'll kill me."

"Tom, why didn't you wake me sooner? Oh, Tom don't! It makes my flesh crawl to hear you. Tom, what is the matter?"

"I forgive you everything, Sid, [Groan.] Everything you've ever done to me. When I'm gone –"

"Oh, Tom, you ain't dying, are you? Don't, Tom – oh, don't. Maybe –"

"I forgive everybody, Sid. [Groan.] Tell 'em so, Sid. And, Sid, you give my window sash and my cat with one eye to that new girl that's come to town, and tell her –"

But Sid had snatched his clothes and gone. (…)

He flew downstairs and said:

"Oh, Aunt Polly, come! Tom's dying!"

"Dying!"

"Yes'm. Don't wait – come quick!"

"Rubbage! I don't believe it!"

But she fled upstairs, nevertheless, with Sid and Mary at her heels. And her face grew white, too, and her lip trembled. When she reached the bedside she gasped out:

"You, Tom! Tom, what's the matter with you?"

"Oh, auntie, I'm –"

"What's the matter with you – what is the matter with you, child?"

"Oh, auntie, my sore toe's mortified!"

The old lady sank down into a chair and laughed a little, then cried a little, then did both together. This restored her and she said:

"Tom, what a turn you did give me. Now you shut up that nonsense and climb out of this."

The groans ceased and the pain vanished from the toe. The boy felt a little foolish, and he said:

"Aunt Polly, it seemed mortified, and it hurt so I never minded my tooth at all."

"Your tooth, indeed! What's the matter with your tooth?"

"One of them's loose, and it aches perfectly awful."

"There, there, now, don't begin the groaning again. Open your mouth. Well, your tooth is loose, but you're not going to die about that. Mary, get me a silk thread, and a chunk of fire out of the kitchen."

Tom said:

"Oh, please, auntie, don't pull it out. It don't hurt any more. I wish I may never stir if it does. Please don't, auntie. I don't want to stay home from school."

"Oh, you don't, don't you? So all this row was because you thought you'd get to stay home from school and go a-fishing? Tom, Tom, I love you so, and you seem to try every way you can to break my old heart with your outrageousness." By this time the dental instruments were ready. The old lady made one end of the silk thread fast to Tom's tooth with a loop and tied the other to the bedpost. Then she seized the chunk of fire and suddenly thrust it almost into the boy's face. The tooth hung dangling by the bedpost, now.

But all trials bring their compensations. As Tom wended to school after breakfast, he was the envy of every boy he met because the gap in his upper row of teeth enabled him to expectorate in a new and admirable way.

(from: The Adventures of Tom Sawyer by Mark Twain)

True/False
Say whether the following statements are true or false. Correct the false statements.

STATEMENTS	True	False
1. Tom likes Monday mornings.		
2. That morning Tom wished he was sick.		
3. One of his lower front teeth was loose.		
4. Tom had a sore finger.		
5. Tom groaned and woke up his sister Sid.		
6. Sid was worried about Tom.		
7. Sid went downstairs and called their grandmother.		
8. Aunt Polly didn't believe that Tom's toe was mortified.		
9. Tom told his aunt about his loose tooth.		
10. Aunt Polly pulled his tooth out.		
11. Tom didn't have to go to school that day.		

Autumn Poems

Homework

I have to write an autumn poem …
'Make it rhyme,' she said,
'If you have time.'
I couldn't be worse
At writing verse.
Tomorrow I have to give it in,
So I'll begin.

An autumn poem
Needs golden sheaves
And swirling leaves
Of orange, purple, red –
and corn – or bread –
For harvest spread.
Ripe acorns abound;
Shiny conkers hit the ground.
I'd better mention laden trees,
Ripe apples shaken by the breeze…
The hedgehog snores,
And diligent squirrel stores,
While swallows leave these shores.
School starts in September:
It's not long till November
With Guy Fawkes to remember.
But spooky Hallowe'en
Comes in between.

Have you written this poem?
Yes, this one's mine. Good. Yes, that's fine.
Now let's do one about Christmas…
Oh no! … 'pheasant, pleasant, present…
Jolly, holly, dolly…'

(Margaret Porter)

Rain

I opened my eyes
And looked up at the rain,
And it dripped in my head
And flowed into my brain,
And all that I hear as I lie in my bed
Is the slishity-slosh of the rain in my head.

I step very softly,
I walk very slow,
I can't do a handstand –
I might overflow,
So pardon the wild crazy thing I just said –
I'm just not the same since there's rain in my head.

(Shel Silverstein)

Apple Harvest

Here are two well-known recipes for British puddings which use apples. They are all served either with cream, vanilla ice-cream, or custard.

Apple pie

Preparation time: 45 minutes
Cooking time: 30 minutes

What you need:
- for the pastry:
  225 g flour
  a little salt
  125 g butter
  4 tablespoons cold water
  a little milk
- for the filling:
  1 kilo apples
  150 g brown sugar

1. Sift flour and salt into a bowl.
2. Cut the butter into small pieces and add to the flour and salt mixture.
3. Rub the butter into the flour until the mixture is like small breadcrumbs.
4. Add the water and knead the pastry until it comes together in a large lump.
5. Put the pastry into the refrigerator for 30 minutes.
6. Peel and slice the apples.
7. Put them in an ovenproof dish.
8. Add the sugar.
9. Roll out the pastry. Make it a little bigger than the top of the dish.
10. Wet the edges of the dish with water.
11. Put the pastry on top of the apples and push the edges of the pastry against the edge of the dish with your thumbs.
12. Brush the top of the pastry with the milk.
13. Bake in a hot oven at 200° C for about 30 minutes.

Eat hot with vanilla ice-cream, cream, or custard.

An apple a day keeps the doctor away.

Apple crumble

Preparation time: 20 minutes
Cooking time: 30 minutes

What you need:
5 big apples
90 g brown sugar
150 g flour
90 g butter
A little cinnamon

1. Peel the apples and cut them into small pieces.
2. Put them in an ovenproof dish.
3. Cut the butter into very small pieces and mix with the flour, sugar and cinnamon.
4. Put this mixture on the apples and bake in a hot oven at 200° C for about half an hour.

Eat warm with cream, ice-cream, or custard.

WEATHER WORDSEARCH

There are twenty-six words in this puzzle which all have something to do with the weather. They can be written forwards, backwards, up, down or diagonally. ↔ ↕ ↘ ↗ Find the hidden words and write them in the spaces next to the puzzle in capital letters. Then use the letters with a circle around them to write a weather poem.

T	O	H	T	H	U	N	D	E	R	W	O	H
F	W	A	U	M	B	R	E	L	L	A	O	E
O	E	I	C	E	H	A	E	D	S	T	N	A
G	L	S	N	I	W	I	N	D	T	E	E	T
N	L	H	S	T	T	N	F	U	O	R	N	G
I	I	O	A	S	E	O	R	P	R	I	A	L
N	N	W	U	T	O	R	N	S	M	E	C	L
T	G	E	T	A	E	F	R	O	S	T	I	C
H	T	R	U	M	U	W	N	I	U	M	R	O
G	O	S	M	O	W	O	B	N	I	A	R	L
I	N	U	N	W	O	N	I	C	L	O	U	D
L	S	I	I	N	D	S	O	L	I	A	H	W
E	A	S	P	R	I	N	G	O	N	U	S	A

Score:
over 25 – excellent
20–25 – good
12–19 – fair

"That's the way the wind blows!"

1. What does the title mean? Explain it in your own words. Use your dictionary.

2. Now try to find the meanings of these expressions in your dictionary. Make a sentence using each of the expressions.
   a) to get wind of something
   b) to run like the wind
   c) to sail close to the wind,
   d) to take the wind out of somebody's sails
   e) to throw caution to the winds
   f) a wind of change
   g) He's full of wind
   h) There's something in the wind

3. Are there any expressions like these in your own language?

Wind and wind belts

Wind is one of the most important features of our weather, together with temperature, clouds and rainfall. When we say "a west wind" we refer to the direction the wind is blowing from, not where it is blowing to.

Winds blow because the sun heats different parts of the atmosphere at different times of the year and depending on whether it is day or night. Air expands when it is heated. It becomes lighter and rises. Cold air flows in to take the place of the warm air. These movements create local wind patterns and also the large "wind belts" around the world.

The most significant wind belts are known as the Prevailing Westerlies, Trades, Polar Easterlies and the Doldrums, a region along the Equator where winds seldom blow.

Do you know the words for these winds in your own language?

The world's "wind belts"

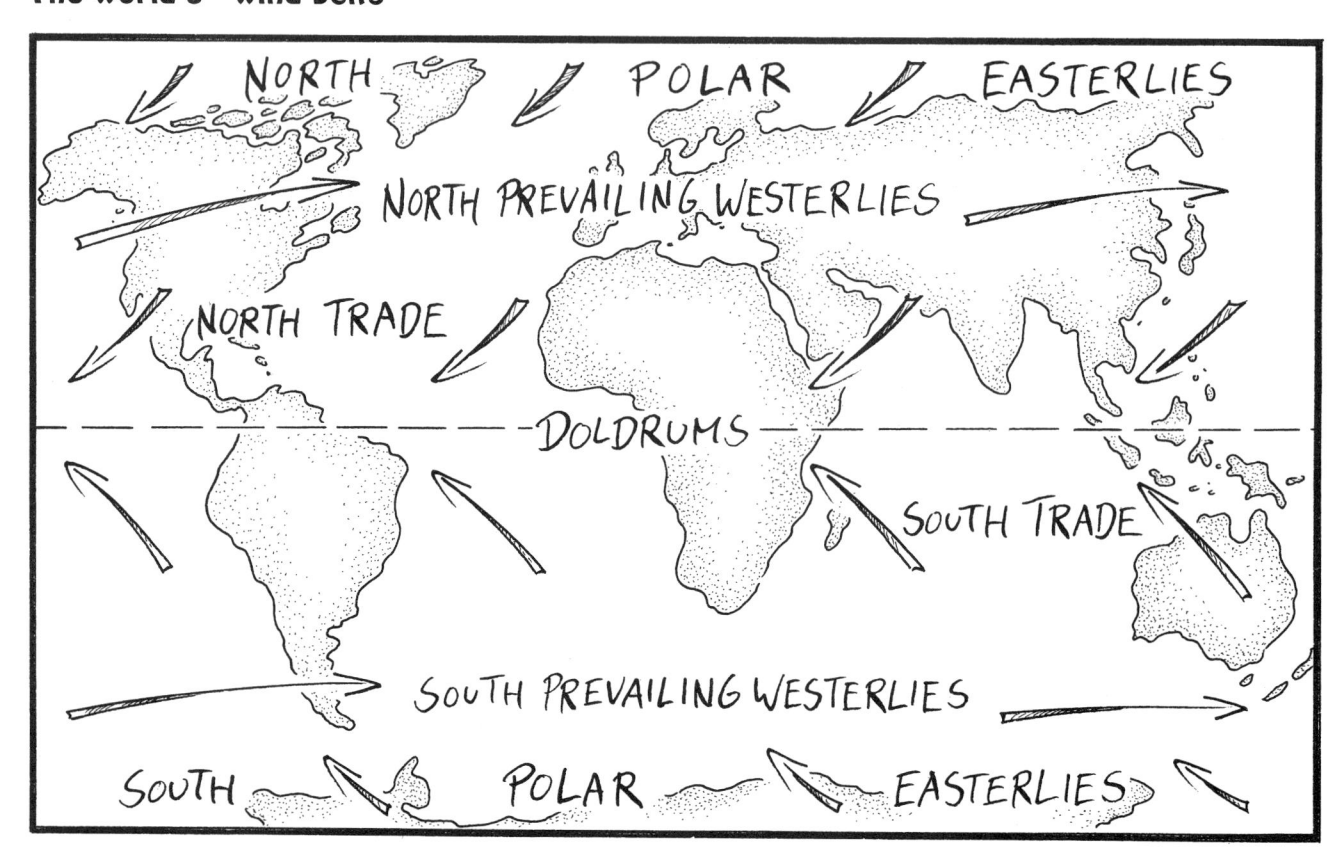

Choose another feature of the weather, (e.g. clouds, rainfall, thunderstorms) and try to describe it in English. Draw diagrams to illustrate your description.

Christopher Columbus and the discovery of America

1. On August 3rd, 1492, Christopher Columbus, an Italian sailor, set sail from Spain in search of a sea route to India. His expedition was paid for by Queen Isabella and King Ferdinand of Spain.

2. America had not yet been discovered and Columbus believed that if he sailed west across the Atlantic ocean he would reach the wealthy Asian countries of the far east.

3. Columbus sailed with three ships, the "Niña", "Pinta" and "Santa Maria". Eighty-eight men were on board the ships.

4. The journey across the Atlantic was long and difficult. The sailors became frightened when they did not find land for so long. There were threats of mutiny.

5. Before dawn, on 12th October 1492, the ships reached an island in the Bahamas. Columbus claimed the land for Spain and called the island "San Salvador". He was disappointed to find a primitive world and not the wealthy Asian civilization he had expected.

6. Back home in Spain, however, Queen Isabella and King Ferdinand were very pleased about Columbus' discovery, a discovery which was to change the history of the whole world. To his death, Columbus believed that he had found the sea route to India, and the natives of America were called "Indians" after Columbus' error. The land Columbus had discovered later became known as "America", after Amerigo Vespucci, who, in 1499, explored the mainland for Portugal.

7. 12th October is Columbus Day in the USA. American people remember the day Christopher Columbus discovered the New World. Many American people display a flag in honour of Christopher Columbus.

8. The biggest celebrations take place in New York with large parades in the streets. Columbus Day is an important celebration for Italian-Americans. This is because Christopher Columbus was an Italian, even though he sailed for the Spanish King and Queen.

It's Hallowe'en

Listening Comprehension

Listen to the text on the cassette and answer the questions about Hallowe'en.

1. When is Hallowe'en?
2. Hallowe'en dates back to Celtic times. What did the Celts celebrate at this time of year?
3. What are the names of the two Christian festivals which come after Hallowe'en?
4. What do you call the hollowed-out pumpkins with faces cut into them which are lit by candles?
5. Where do young people usually go in the evenings at Hallowe'en?
6. How do children and young people dress up at Hallowe'en?
7. How do Hallowe'en evenings in the USA usually end?
8. Explain what "trick or treat" means.

Hallowe'en Wordsearch

Find the following "Hallowe'en" words in the wordsearch puzzle:

All Saints' Day   All Souls' Day   bonfires   candles   candy   evil   fun
ghosts   goblins   jack-o-lantern   masks   October   parties   pumpkins
spirits   spooky   superstition   trick or treat   witches

```
A ☺ I J N S O S D I X A D V T K P V J U
O H C T F F A L L ☺ S A I N T S' ☺ D A Y
C D N M U Z L B C E U B E O R V Q R C A
T G C A N D L E S C P D E V I L U M K P
O N A R E V ☺ B P E E F U S C D Z L ☺ K
B R N P P A S B O H R W M B K C W C O' I
E F D C U C O E O H S R A J ☺ G I T ☺ I
R H Y L M T U K K I T K S J O A T S L Z
Y U W D P Q L X Y A I B K S R D C R A E
S Q G F K L S' J G L T G S J ☺ W H B N Q
P ☺ O P I M ☺ L L A I K I E T H E P T F
I V B D N U D Y C B O N F I R E S G E Y
R O L V S Y A R F Z N Y S X E J H H R X
I W I G M Z Y E O T W T W T X A L O K N A
T B N D ☺ N O P M Q S P A R T I E S U V
S G S Q G H O S T S M X R W N M N F X ☺
```

Guy Fawkes' Night – 5th November

Thanksgiving – Fourth Thursday in November (USA)

About Thanksgiving Day
Write these words in the correct places in the text.

climate   corn   dinner   diseases   farmers   food   fourth   half   harvest   Mayflower   parades   Plymouth   pumpkin pie   survive   sweet potatoes   together   tribes   turkey   voyage   winter

Thanksgiving is celebrated in the USA on the _____ Thursday in November. It commemorates the first Thanksgiving in 1621 which was celebrated in _____ , New England by the Pilgrims, new settlers from England who had arrived there a year before.

The Pilgrims left Plymouth in England in September 1620 on their ship, the _____ . After a long and hard _____ they finally landed at a place on the North American coast, which they called Plymouth, New England. The first _____ was very hard for the Pilgrims. They were not very good _____ and the plants and seeds they had brought with them did not flourish in the rough _____ of New England. There was not enough _____ , the winter was hard and there were _____ . More than _____ of the settlers died.

In the second year the local Indian _____ helped the Pilgrims with their spring planting of native crops like _____ and _____ _____ . After their first successful _____ that autumn they had a big Thanksgiving feast, together with the Indians who had helped them to _____ . Nowadays Thanksgiving is celebrated with colourful _____ . The biggest one takes place along Central Park West in New York. But above all, Thanksgiving is a day for families to come _____ . There is usually a big _____ with _____ , corn, sweet potatoes and other vegetables and _____ _____ .

Questions
1. Where and when was the first Thanksgiving celebration?
2. Who were the Pilgrims?
3. Why did so many of them die in their first winter in New England?
4. How and why did the situation change in the pilgrim's second year?
5. What happens on Thanksgiving Day in the USA nowadays?

CHRISTMAS: FACTS, FUN AND FAITH

Did you know???

In Britain Christmas time is a time of fun and merrymaking. People decorate their homes with paper chains and balloons. Shops, banks, offices, restaurants, etc. are decorated too.

The first Christmas cards were printed in 1843. The man who invented them was called Sir Henry Coles, the first director of the Victoria and Albert Museum in London. Only 1,000 copies were produced. Today millions of Christmas cards are sent each year. People in Britain and the USA put the cards they receive on the mantlepiece or hang them on the walls. Many people buy charity Christmas cards. The most popular producer of charity cards is UNICEF.

In 1840 Prince Albert, the German-born husband of Queen Victoria, first introduced the Christmas tree decorated with candles, tinsel and ornaments to the Royal Family's Christmas. Soon the Christmas tree was popular throughout the whole of Britain. Nowadays electric fairy lights are used rather than candles.

Before Christmas in the evenings, groups of people go from house to house singing Christmas carols. They are usually raising money for charity.

Before Christmas young children in Britain and America send letters to Father Christmas or Santa Claus, listing the presents they would like to receive. Very young children believe that Father Christmas comes on Christmas Eve in the night, flying on a sleigh pulled by reindeer. They think he climbs down the chimney and fills their stockings with presents. Children open their presents on Christmas Day.

In the old days churches had "Alms Boxes" which people could put presents or money for the poor into on Christmas Day. The day after Christmas these boxes were opened and the presents were distributed among the poor people. This is why the day after Christmas became known as Boxing Day. Later people gave presents or money in "Christmas boxes" to their servants on Boxing Day. Today some people, such as postwomen and postmen, are given a "Christmas box" to thank them for their services throughout the year.

Pantomimes are popular at Christmas time in Britain. A pantomime is a comedy and is entertainment for the whole family. It is a play often based on a popular fairy tale in which, the main male character is played by a woman and the main female character is played by a man. There is always a "baddie", who people boo or hiss at.

The traditional British Christmas dinner consists of roast turkey, roast potatoes and Brussels sprouts followed by Christmas pudding. Christmas cake is a rich fruit cake which was traditionally made on "Stir up Sunday" the last Sunday before Advent. Christmas pudding, or plum pudding, was steamed for three hours on Christmas Day. Christmas in Britain would not be complete without mince pies, little pies filled with mincemeat, which is a spicy mixture of raisins, sultanas, currants, candied peel, almonds, suet, apple and sherry. People in Britain only eat mince pies at Christmas. You can eat them hot or cold, on their own or with cream. Nowadays most people buy their mince pies and Christmas puddings at the supermarket and heat them up in the oven or in the microwave at home. Superstitious people believe that eating mince pies brings you luck. According to a saying "one mince pie every day from Christmas to Twelfth Night brings twelve happy months."

At Christmas time people make door and table decorations with holly and mistletoe: plants which are green even when it is cold outside.

Kissing under the mistletoe goes back to Celtic times. For the Celts mistletoe was a symbol of fertility. Nowadays bunches of mistletoe are often hung up in schools and offices and when two people meet under them they have to kiss each other! The holly wreath hung on the front door originated in the USA.

In Australia Christmas is in the summer holidays. People often eat Christmas dinner on the beach. Some people even take their Christmas tree and crackers with them! Christmas picnics usually consist of cold turkey (or chicken or roast beef) with salad. On Christmas Eve Australian people meet in city parks to sing Christmas carols. Thousands of people take part in these events and the parks are beautifully illuminated with candles.

The Giant Christmas Crossword

Across ➡

4. A special kind of Christmas play, often based on a fairytale. (9)
6. The animal which pulls Father Christmas's sleigh. (8)
7. Mr Claus's first name. (5)
9. People hang these up in their houses at Christmas. (8)
12. These things have jokes, paper hats and a small gift in them! (8)
13. Prickly, green plant with red berries. (5)
16. Usually only found outside, but at Christmas most homes have one inside, too. (4)
18. Looks like an angel. You put it on top of the Christmas tree.
19. You put this around presents to make them look nice and so that people don't know what's inside. (8)
21. The other half of 7. across. (5)
23. According to the Bible, what the three wise Kings followed to get to Bethlehem. (4)
24. Something which makes a ringing sound. (4)
25. You can tie this around a present. (6)
26. Special Christmas pies in Britain are called … pies. (5)
27. What people put on their Christmas trees instead of candles. (6)
28. Take the end of "Mississippi" and the beginning of "especially" and you've got some things which people in Britain enjoy eating! (4)
29. Usually made of holly and hung on the door at Christmas. (6)

Down ⬇

1. Made of wax, originally used as a light on a Christmas tree. (6)
2. Old fashioned word for sock. Children hang them up on Christmas Eve for Father Christmas to put their presents into. (8)
3. The bed – in the stable – which Jesus was said to lie in. (4)
4. British and American children open these on Christmas Day. (7)
5. If you stand under this at Christmas you might get kissed! (9)
8. Most important part of the main course of a traditional British Christmas dinner. (6)
10. Traditionally at Christmas in England this is very sweet and covered in marzipan and icing. (4)
11. Plural noun from the verb 'to decorate'. (11)
12. A girl's name and a Christmas song. (5)
14. What this crossword is all about! (9)
15. It's a round, shiny decoration for a Christmas tree. (6)
17. Anagram of 'glean'. It has wings and sings! (5)
20. Turn 'it' upside down then add north, south, east and left – and you've got something to put on your Christmas tree. (6)
21. British and American people send hundreds of these at Christmas. (5)
22. Add the French for 'the' to a 'sigh' and you've got Santa's vehicle! (6)

Christmas jokes

Knock! Knock!
Who's there?
Mary!
Mary who?
Mary* Christmas!

(*Mary sounds like 'merry'!)

Knock! Knock!
Who's there?
Anna!
Anna who?
Anna* Happy New Year!

(*Anna sounds like 'and a'!)

Knock! Knock!
Who's there?
Ivor!
Ivor who?
Ivor gotten* your Christmas presents!

(*'Ivor gotten' sounds like 'I've forgotten'!)

Son: "I know that Father Christmas doesn't really exist."
Mother: "Why do you say that?"
Son: "Because the Easter Bunny told me."

Music lover: "How much do you charge to sing Christmas carols?"
Billy: "Twenty pence, sir."
Music lover: "And how much do you charge not to sing?"
Billy: "Fifty pence, sir!"
Music lover: "Well, here's a fiver. Leave me in peace for ten years."

Bob: "Some carol singers came to my house late last night. I had to open the door in my pyjamas."
Malcolm: "That's a funny place to have a door."

The carol singers knocked on the door and when the owner answered it, they burst into Silent Night.
"Do you know it's five to midnight on Christmas Eve?" said the angry man.
"No!" replied one of the singers. "But if you hum it slowly we'll all join in."

Customer in a posh restaurant:
"Do your serve turkey at Christmas, sir?"
Waiter: "Only if it's properly dressed, sir."

Ken: "Mum, I don't want to go back to school after the Christmas holidays."
Mum: "You have to darling. After all, you are the headmaster."

Paul: "I wish I had ten pence for every girl I've kissed under the mistletoe this Christmas."
Jenny: "What would you buy? A packet of crisps?"

Customer: "Do you have turkey legs?"
Butcher: "No, madam! It's just the way I'm standing."

Billy: "What's the difference between tree decorations and rotten fish?"
Rosie: "I don't know."
Billy: "So that's why your Christmas tree smells so bad!"

Christmas crackers

In 1840 Tom Smith, the owner of a London sweet shop, went to Paris. He was very impressed by the way French confectioners wrapped their sweets in twists of coloured paper. Tom Smith copied the idea and it soon became very popular in London to give beautifully wrapped sweets as presents. Later Tom Smith began to put love mottoes, jokes or riddles inside the sweets. Eventually he invented the cracker as it is known in Britain today. In each cracker he hid a small gift, a paper hat and a motto, riddle or joke. He then treated two pieces of cardboard with chemicals to make a small bang – or crack – when the cracker was pulled apart. Tom Smith's idea became so popular that he opened a factory in 1847 and there is still a Tom Smith cracker factory in Norwich today.

Make your own crackers
These crackers don't crack – but they do make a nice present for your family and friends.

You need:
- coloured crêpe paper or christmas wrapping paper
- cardboard tube from 1 toilet roll for each cracker + 1 extra tube
- cotton, coloured string or tinsel
- small christmas stickers (e. g. stars) or glitter
- one small gift for each cracker
- one motto, riddle or joke for each cracker, printed on a small piece of paper.

To make:
1. Cut a paper crown out of crepe paper. Stick it together and fold it up to fit in the cracker.

2. Cut one of the toilet rolls into 4 equal parts

3. Put the whole roll and two of the parts on to the crêpe paper:

4. Cut the paper to the length of the 3 tubes and wide enough to roll round them with approximately 1½ cms extra to overlap.

5. Put your gift, hat and joke into the large tube.

6. Stick the crêpe paper to the middle tube. Then stick the paper together at the ends, but do not stick it to the tubes.

7. Carefully tie cotton, coloured string or tinsel at each end of the middle tube where the tubes meet.

8. Remove the small pieces of tube from the ends.

9. Decorate the cracker with stickers, glitter, holly, etc.

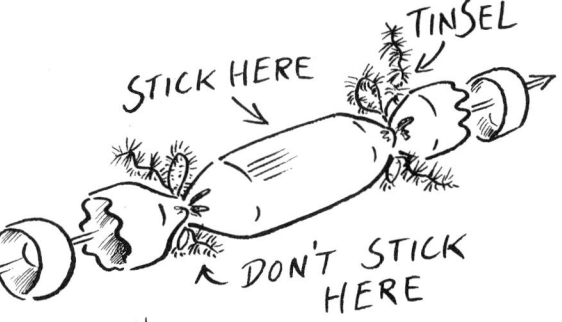

Nick's thank you letter

Nick's thank you letter is written in a code. Can you work it out?
1. Write out the letter in real words. 2. Write your own coded letter.

Happy "Chinese" New Year!

Chinese New Year is on a different date each year. It is usually between the middle of January and late February. It is the most important festival for Chinese families all over the world. Every year in the Chinese calendar is named after a different animal. According to a Chinese legend the gods arranged a race between twelve animals. The first year in the sequence was given the name of the winning animal. For most of the race the ox was in the lead, but the clever rat jumped on his back and jumped off as the ox approached the finish. And so the first year in the sequence is the year of the rat. The rest of the sequence is given below.

1. Which animal is this year the year of?
2. Fill in the years in the "Chinese Calendar" given below.
3. Which animal rules the year you (your parents, your brothers and sisters, grandparents, friends) were born?
4. Look at the characteristics assigned to the people born in particular years. What do you think of them? Do they fit people you know who were born in these years? Do you believe in this kind of thing?

YEARS OF

People born under this sign are said to be

THE RAT
1900, _____
_____
_____

charming, kind, cheerful, ambitious, full of integrity, good at making friends.

THE OX
1901, _____
_____
_____

quiet, patient, strong, faithful, warm, stubborn, good at listening to others.

THE TIGER
1902, _____
_____
_____

brave, intelligent, powerful, respected by others.

YEARS OF

People born under this sign are said to be

THE HARE
1903, _____
_____
_____

lucky, happy, good-tempered, successful.

THE DRAGON
1904, _____
_____
_____

healthy, energetic, gentle, honest, courageous, good rulers.

THE SNAKE
1905, _____
_____
_____

beautiful, wise, careful, fortunate in money matters.

YEARS OF

People born under this sign are said to be

THE HORSE
1906, _____
_____
_____

cheerful, popular, quick-witted, talented, impulsive, good with their hands.

THE RAM
1907, _____
_____
_____

artistic, creative, sincere, compassionate, shy, fond of beautiful things.

THE MONKEY
1908, _____
_____
_____

clever, creative, successful, well-informed, selfish, vain, good at making decisions.

YEARS OF

People born under this sign are said to be

THE ROOSTER
1909, _____
_____
_____

upright, outspoken, alert, precise, proud, inclined to express themselves in music or writing.

THE DOG
1910, _____
_____
_____

loyal, honest, discreet, straightforward, conscientious, good friends to have.

THE PIG
1911, _____
_____
_____

straightforward, honest, courteous, shy, brave, good at making friendships for life.

Snow

Baked Alaska
This is an ice-cream and cake dessert.
It's hot and cold and is perfect for a winter's day.

You need:
20 cm round sponge cake
250 ml tinned raspberries (or other fruit)
drained juice from tinned fruit
475 g ice-cream
4 egg whites
165 g sugar

Heat the oven to 230°C. Put the cake on a baking tray. Pour some fruit juice over the cake. Use a spoon and put the ice-cream onto the middle of the cake. Leave a small gap around the cake uncovered. Put the fruit on top of the ice-cream. Put the cake into the freezer.
Now you need to make the meringue. Beat the egg whites until they are stiff. Then beat in the sugar, one spoonful at a time, until the egg white stands in stiff peaks. Take the cake out of the freezer and cover it with the meringue. The meringue must completely cover the cake, the ice cream, and the fruit, as well as completely covering the sides. Put the cake in the oven. Take it out when the meringue begins to look brown.

Eat your Baked Alaska immediately!

A tongue twister

Shelly saw six slimy slugs
Snuggling in slushy snow.

Death of a Snowman

I was awake all night
Big as a polar bear
Strong and firm and white.
The tall black hat I wear
Was draped with ermine fur.
I felt so fit and well
Till the world began to stir
And the morning sun swell.
I was tired, began to yawn;
At noon in the humming sun
I caught a severe warm;
My nose began to run.
My hat grew black and fell,
Was followed by my grey head.
There was no funeral bell,
But by tea-time I was dead.

(Vernon Scannell)

1. Who is the speaker of this poem supposed to be?
2. What was on his head?
3. When did he feel well?
4. Why does he say he caught a severe warm? (What illness can people catch?)
5. Describe the scene at the end of the poem.

MARTIN LUTHER KING DAY

About Martin Luther King
Listen to the information and note down the facts about Martin Luther King's life.

1. Born: When? Where? _____

2. College: Name? At what age? _____

3. University: Name? _____

4. 1947: _____

5. Wife: Name? Year of marriage? _____

6. Children: How many? _____

7. First pastorship: Where? _____

8. First success against racial discrimination: Where? _____

   What? _____

9. August 28, 1963: _____

10. 1964: _____

11. April 4, 1968 _____

12. Since 1986, third Monday in January: _____

Use your notes and write down what you know about Martin Luther King. You may need a separate sheet of paper.

_____
_____
_____
_____
_____
_____
_____
_____
_____
_____

14th February – Valentine's Day

Listening comprehension

Listen to the information and answer these questions about Valentine's Day.

1. Who is St Valentine the patron saint of?
2. There were two Roman saints called Valentine. Which century did they live in?
3. What did the two St Valentines have in common?
4. What was Lupercalia?
5. What was a typical custom at the festival of Lupercalia?
6. In which century was Valentine's Day first celebrated in Britain?
7. What was so special about the presents which British people used to leave outside their friends' and relatives' front doors?
8. Who was Queen when exchanging cards on Valentine's Day became very popular for the first time?
9. When did Queen Victoria reign?
10. Sending cards did not always remain popular. When was the custom taken up again?
11. Name at least three symbols which commonly appear on Valentine cards.
12. Who was Venus?
13. Who was Cupid?
14. What could Cupid do with his special arrows?
15. What do Valentine cards often have inside them?
16. When did the tradition of celebrating Valentine's Day begin in North America?
17. State two things which the early settlers in North America used to do before Valentine's Day.
18. Give two reasons why Valentine's Day was so important for the early settlers in North America.

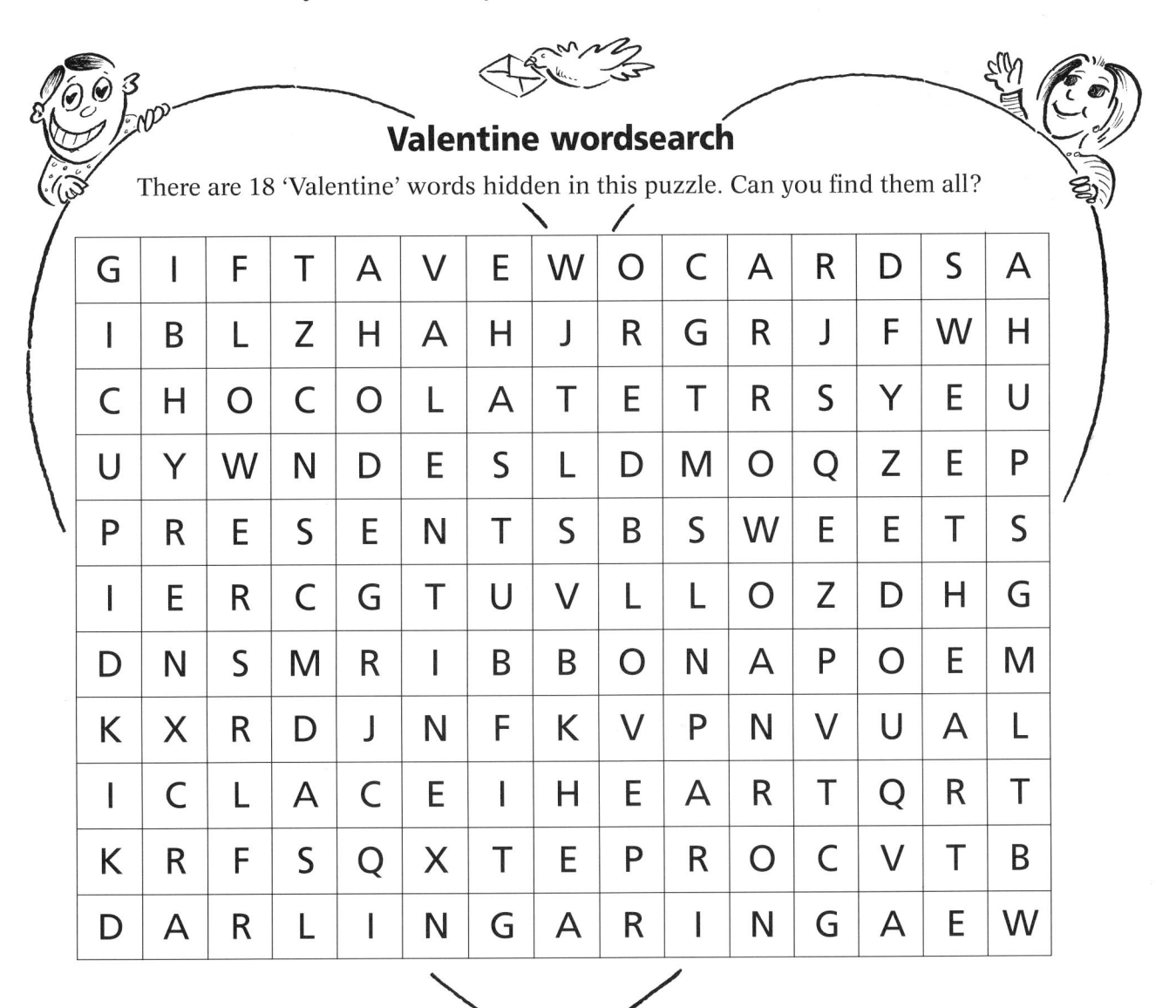

Valentine wordsearch

There are 18 'Valentine' words hidden in this puzzle. Can you find them all?

G	I	F	T	A	V	E	W	O	C	A	R	D	S	A
I	B	L	Z	H	A	H	J	R	G	R	J	F	W	H
C	H	O	C	O	L	A	T	E	T	R	S	Y	E	U
U	Y	W	N	D	E	S	L	D	M	O	Q	Z	E	P
P	R	E	S	E	N	T	S	B	S	W	E	E	T	S
I	E	R	C	G	T	U	V	L	L	O	Z	D	H	G
D	N	S	M	R	I	B	B	O	N	A	P	O	E	M
K	X	R	D	J	N	F	K	V	P	N	V	U	A	L
I	C	L	A	C	E	I	H	E	A	R	T	Q	R	T
K	R	F	S	Q	X	T	E	P	R	O	C	V	T	B
D	A	R	L	I	N	G	A	R	I	N	G	A	E	W

6.1

67

President's Day

On President's Day people in the USA honour two of their greatest presidents: Abraham Lincoln and George Washington. President's Day is celebrated on the third Monday in February.
Read the information below about the two presidents. Use your dictionary to help you with any new vocabulary. Why do you think President's Day is celebrated on the third Monday in February?

About George Washington
(22nd February 1732-14th December 1799)

George Washington is often called "The Father of His Country" because he was the first president of the United States of America. He was born on 22nd February, 1732, in Westmoreland County, Virginia. He studied mathe-
5 matics and geography and became a surveyor at the age of 17.
During the American War of Independence (1775-1883) he led the American soldiers against the British army. After eight years of fighting the American revolutionary
10 army won the war and the thirteen British colonies became the United States of America. George Washington was elected the first president. The capital of the United States, Washington D.C., is named after him. George Washington is regarded by many Americans as a man of
15 particular honesty. There is a famous story about him and his fondness for telling the truth, which is known by every American child. The story goes that, when George was a young boy, he cut down a cherry tree in his father's garden. When his father asked him who had cut the tree down George could easily have denied doing it, but
20 instead, he looked into his father's eyes and declared: "I cannot tell a lie, Father, I cut down the cherry tree." Nowadays in many families in the USA it has become a tradition to serve Cherry Cobbler, a delicious pudding made with cherries, in honour of George Washington on President's Day.

About Abraham Lincoln
(12th February 1809 – 15th April 1865)

Abraham Lincoln, the American president famous for his intelligence and insight, was born in a log cabin in Kentucky on 12th February 1809. His father was a frontiersman who hunted and did a little farming. His mother took care of the cabin and the children. When Abraham was nine years old 5 his mother died.
As a child and young man Abraham spent many evenings by the fireside reading books and teaching himself many things. He was particularly interested in law. He did many jobs when he was young: he split rails, worked as a postmaster 10 and was a clerk in a general store in the local town.
At the age of 22 Abraham Lincoln and his family moved to Illinois. He became a successful lawyer there. He was interested in politics, and, in 1834, he was elected to the Illinois House of Representatives. Later he became Senator of 15 the state of Illinois. In 1860 he was elected the 16th president of the United States. He believed that all people ought to be free and he opposed slavery. He was a man of great speeches. He gave his best known speech, the "Gettysburg Address" on the battlefield of Gettysburg during the American Civil War (1861-1865). Ten days after the end of that war, on 14th April, 1865, Lincoln was shot by an assassin, and died the next day. 20
Everyone in America knows what Lincoln looked like because his face is featured on the smallest US coin, the copper penny. There is also a huge marble building in Washington D.C., the Lincoln Memorial, where crowds of people go everyday to look at Lincoln's statue.

President's Day

On the third Monday in February people in America
celebrate the birthdays of two of their greatest presidents:
George Washington, whose birthday was on 22nd February and
Abraham Lincoln, whose birthday was on 12th February.

Tick (✔) which president the statements are true for: George Washington or Abraham Lincoln.

George Washington or Abraham Lincoln?

	George Washington	Abraham Lincoln
1. The capital of the USA is named after him.		
2. He became famous for his wit and insight.		
3. He was born in Kentucky.		
4. He was born in 1732.		
5. He was the first president of the United States.		
6. He was assassinated on 14th April, 1865.		
7. He was born in Virginia.		
8. His face is printed on the American copper penny.		
9. He is often called "The Father of Our Country".		
10. He was a successful lawyer.		
11. As a young boy, he cut down his father's cherry tree.		
12. He was Commander of the American army during the War of Independence.		
13. He opposed slavery.		
14. He studied mathematics and geography.		
15. He was born in 1809.		
16. When he was a child he lived in a log cabin.		
17. He was interested in many things, especially in reading.		
18. At the age of 17 he became a surveyor.		
19. He liked reading.		
20. He was the 16th president of the USA.		

Pancake Day

Pancake?
Who wants a pancake,
Sweet and piping hot?
Good little Grace looks up and says,
"I'll take the one on the top."
Who else wants a pancake,
Fresh off the griddle?
Terrible Theresa smiles and says,
"I'll take the one in the middle."

(Shel Silverstein)

Pancake Day falls in February. This festival has got different names in different countries, and there are various ways of celebrating it.

Unscramble the following text to create four paragraphs with the headings **Shrove Tuesday, Pancake Day, Carnival** and **Mardi Gras.**

If a pancake lands in the road, the racer is allowed to pick it up and toss it again! It is uncertain whether the pancakes are eaten at the end of the race! Because, on the day before the beginning of Lent, people used to go to church to confess all the things they had done wrong and ask God to forgive them. This was known as "shriving", and "shrove" comes from shriving. And in the past Christian people gave up eating meat during Lent because they believed that Jesus did not eat at all during this time. Local specialities are sold in the streets: oysters, crabs, deep-fried sweet pastries and gumbo, a typical Creole dish. So, the day before Lent began, people used up all the eggs, fat and milk they still had in the house by making pancakes. New Orleans on Louisiana's Gulf coast is famous for its Mardi Gras celebrations. Today people in Britain traditionally eat pancakes with lemon juice and sugar on Pancake Day, though pancakes are rarely eaten at any other time of the year! According to the rules all competitors must live in the village. Two of the most famous carnivals in the world are the Rio Carnival in Rio de Janeiro, Brazil, and Mardi Gras in New Orleans. The most famous race takes place in Olney, a village in Buckinghamshire, and this tradition is more than 500 years old. The word "carnival" comes from the Latin "carnem levare" which means "to take away meat". They must wear aprons and have hats or scarves on their heads. Carnival was a time for having fun before the forty days of fasting and prayer began. All sorts of games were played in the streets to celebrate. The pancakes have to be tossed three times during the race before they reach the church. In many countries nowadays it is a time for dressing up in masks and costumes and having parties and dancing. In some countries the celebrations start at the beginning of January and last until Ash Wednesday, the first day of Lent. There are parades and everyone dances in masks to the sound of jazz bands. In Quebec City, Canada, the winter carnival celebrations last eleven days. They include parades and special sporting events, such as skating, skiing, tobogganning and canoe races through the freezing waters of the St. Lawrence river. Carnival, as such, is not celebrated in Britain. Mardi Gras is French and means "Fat Tuesday". This is because in the Middle Ages Lent was a time of fasting and people were not allowed to eat rich food, such as fat, eggs or milk until Easter. And the festival was introduced there by the French colonialists. Shrove Tuesday is the last Tuesday before Lent, the forty days leading up to Easter. Why is it called Shrove Tuesday? People from all over the world go to New Orleans to celebrate Mardi Gras. Pancake races are held in several places in England on Pancake Day. It is a thick bitter-sweet tasting soup made of shellfish, okra, onions, herbs and hot pepper. Shrove Tuesday is also popularly called Pancake Day. They gather in the village square, each one holding a frying pan with a cooked pancake in it. When the Pancake Bell is rung they start running in the direction of the parish church.

Can you explain the term "Mardi Gras"?
How are the last days before Lent celebrated in your country?

PADDY'S GREEN SHAMROCK SHORE

(trad.)

This is a song about the famine in Ireland 1840. In those days most of the Irish people lived on potatoes. In 1845, the potato crop was killed by a plant disease and the potato famine began. In 1845 the population of Ireland was eight million. In 1858, the population had diminished to four million. One and a half million people had died. The rest had emigrated, mostly to America.

1. From Derry quay we sailed away
   On the 23rd of May …
   We were boarded by a pleasant crew,
   Bound for Americay;
   Fresh water there we did take on
   Five thousand gallons or more,
   In case we'd run short going to New York
   Far away from the Shamrock Shore

   Chorus:
   *So fare thee well, sweet Lisa dear
   And love on to Derry town;
   And a kind farewell to my comrade boys,
   Who dwell on that sacred ground.
   If fortune should ever favour me,
   And I to have money in store,
   I'll go back and I'll wed the wee lassie I left
   On Paddy's Green Shamrock Shore.*

2. We sailed three days, we were all sea-sick,
   Not a man on board was free;
   We were all confined unto our bunks,
   With no one to pity poor me.
   No father or mother dear kind,
   To lift up my head when 'twas sore,
   Which made me think more on the lassie I left
   On Paddy's Green Shamrock Shore.

   Chorus

3. We safely reached the other side
   In three and twenty days;
   We were taken as prisoners by a man
   Who led us around in three different ways.
   We each of us drank a parting glass
   In case we might meet no more,
   We drank to our health and Ireland
   And Paddy's Green Shamrock Shore.

1. When and from where did the singer leave Ireland?
2. What were the people on board like?
3. Where were they heading for?
4. What will the man do if he ever has enough money?
5. How many of the men were seasick on the journey?
6. Who was there to look after them?
7. How long did the journey take?
8. What did the men do before going their separate ways?
9. Can you think of a heading for each of the verses and the chorus?
10. Can you write the story of the song again in your own words?
11. a) Has anyone in your class come to your country from a different country?
    b) What reasons do people have for emigrating today?

The long winter

This is a true story about an American family snowed in by storms and blizzards lasting seven long months. Their town is completely cut off on the frozen, endless prairie. No trains can reach them to bring food or fuel for the stove. There is no meat left, no butter, only a little fat – meat dripping to spread on bread. And a very small amount of flour – enough for one more baking.
But, as they find, winter never lasts for ever …

'Winter had lasted so long that it seemed it would never end. It seemed that they would never really wake up.
In the morning Laura got out of bed into the cold. She dressed downstairs by the fire that Pa had kindled before he went to the stable. They ate their coarse brown bread. Then all day long she and Ma and Mary ground wheat and twisted hay as fast as they could (it was the only fuel they had to burn on the fire.)
The fire must not go out; it was very cold. They ate some coarse brown bread. Then Laura crawled into the cold bed and shivered until she grew warm enough to sleep.
Next morning she got out of bed into the cold. She dressed in the chilly kitchen by the fire. She ate her coarse brown bread. She took her turns at grinding wheat and twisting hay. But she did not ever feel awake. She felt beaten by the cold and the storms. She knew she was dull and stupid but she could not wake up.
There were no more lessons. There was nothing in the world but cold and dark and work and coarse brown bread and winds blowing. The storm was always there, outside the walls, waiting sometimes, then pouncing, shaking the house, roaring, snarling and screaming in rage.
Out of bed in the morning to hurry down and dress by the fire. Then work all day to crawl into a cold bed at night and fall asleep as soon as she grew warm. The winter had lasted so long. It would never end.
Pa did not sing his trouble song in the mornings any more. On clear days he hauled hay. Sometimes a blizzard lasted only two days. There might be three days of clear cold, or even four days, before the blizzard struck again. 'We're outwearing it,' Pa said.
'It hasn't got much more time. March is nearly gone. We can last longer than it can.'

'The wheat is holding out,' Ma said. 'I am thankful for that.'
The end of March came. April began. Still the storm was there, waiting a little longer now perhaps but striking even more furiously. There was the bitter cold still, and the dark storm days, the wheat to be ground, the hay to be twisted. Laura seemed to have forgotten summer; she could not believe it would come again. April was going by …
'It can't beat us!' Pa said.
'Can't it, Pa?' Laura asked stupidly.
'No,' said Pa. 'It's got to quit sometime and we don't. It can't lick us. We won't give up.'
Then Laura felt a warmth inside her. It was very small but it was strong. It was steady, like a tiny light in the dark, and it burned very low but no winds could make it flicker because it would not give up.
They ate the coarse brown bread and went through the dark and cold upstairs to bed. Shivering in the cold bed Laura and Mary silently said their prayers and slowly grew warm enough to sleep.
Sometime in the night Laura heard the wind. It was still blowing furiously but there were no voices, no howls or shrieks in it. And with it there was another sound, a tiny, uncertain liquid sound that she could not understand.
She listened as hard as she could. She uncovered her ear to listen and the cold did not bite her cheek. The dark was warmer. She put out her hand and felt only a coolness. The little sound that she heard was a trickling of waterdrops. The eaves were dripping. Then she knew.
She sprang up in bed and called aloud, 'Pa! Pa! The Chinook is blowing!'
'I hear it, Laura,' Pa answered from the other room. 'Spring has come. Go back to sleep.'
The Chinook was blowing. Spring had come. The blizzard had given up; it was driven back to the north. Blissfully Laura stretched out in bed; she put both arms on top of the quilts and they were not very cold. She listened to the blowing wind and dripping eaves and she knew that in the other room Pa was lying awake, too, listening and glad. The Chinook, the wind of spring, was blowing. Winter was ended.'

(From *The Long Winter* by Laura Ingalls Wilder)

Tasks
1. Use a dictionary or encyclopaedia and find out what a blizzard and the Chinook is.
2. Approximately which century/year do you think the story takes place in?
   Are there any hints in the text?
3. What time of year does the story take place in? Quote from the text.
4. Where do you think the story takes place? Find clues in the text.
5. Work out what difficulties people had to face in winter.
   What are common features of the end of winter?
6. What is winter like in the area where you live? What is typical about the beginning of spring?

SNOWMAN

'Twas the first day of the springtime,
And the snowman stood alone
As the winter snows were melting,
And the pine trees seemed to groan,
"Ah, you poor sad smiling snowman,
You'll be melting by and by."
Said the snowman, "What a pity,
For I'd like to see July.
Yes, I'd like to see July, and please don't ask me why.
But I'd like to, yes I'd like to, oh I'd like to see July."

Chirped a robin, just arriving,
"Seasons come and seasons go,
And the greatest ice must crumble
When it's flowers' time to grow.
And as one thing is beginning
So another thing must die,
And there's never been a snowman
Who has ever seen July.
No, they never see July, no matter how they try.
No, they never ever, never ever, never see July."

But the snowman sniffed his carrot nose
And said, "At least I'll try."
And he bravely smiled his frosty smile
And blinked his coal-black eye.
And there he stood and faced the sun
A blazin' from the sky –
And I really cannot tell you
If he ever saw July.
Did he ever see July? You can guess as well as I
If he ever, if he never, if he ever saw July.

(Shel Silverstein)

How does the snowman feel on the first day of spring? Why?
How do you feel when spring comes?
Which of the four seasons do you prefer? Why?

The first day of spring

About equinoxes and seasons

21st March is the first day of spring and is also known as the spring equinox. Equinoxes occur twice a year: on the 21st March and on the 22nd September (the autumn equinox). On both of these days the sun's position is directly over the equator and so the hours of daylight are exactly equal to the hours of darkness.

The spring equinox marks the beginning of spring and the autumn equinox marks the first day of autumn.

Seasons occur because the Earth rotates around the Sun at an angle so that the northern and southern hemispheres are alternately tilted towards it or away from it. In the northern hemisphere spring is in the early months of the year, whilst at the same time it is autumn in the southern hemisphere (and vice versa).

In some parts of the world (the tropics) there are only two seasons: a rainy season and a dry season.

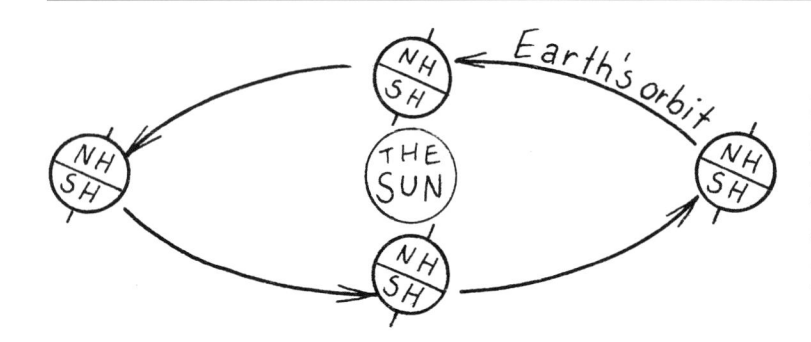

NH: Northern hemisphere
SH: Southern hemisphere
Earth's orbit: 365.25 days in a year
The Earth's axis is tilted at an angle of 23.5°. This position does not change as the Earth travels around the sun.

NH: _____

NH: _____   NH: _____
SH: _____   SH: _____

21st March

21st June   **sun**   **21st December**

22nd September

NH: _____   NH: _____
SH: _____   SH: _____

NH: _____

Label the diagram correctly to show:

a) When the spring and autumn equinoxes occur in the northern hemisphere (NH).
b) When the four seasons occur in the northern and southern hemispheres (SH).

Gardens, gardening and land use

A survey

Spring is the time when many people start work in their gardens again after the winter.
Work in groups and carry out the survey. Then report your findings back to your class.
You may need to go to your local library or local authority to find out some of the information.

Find out:
- how many people in your group have a garden.
- how big people's gardens are and work out the average size of a garden for your group.
- who does most of the gardening in each family.
- how many pupils help in the garden and what they do (or have to do!).
- what people grow in their gardens: fruit, vegetables, flowers, etc.
  Write down the different names and look the English words up in your dictionary.
- whether anyone keeps chickens or any other animals which provide food for the family.
- what crop, fruit and vegetables are grown on farms in your area.
- what kind of soil predominates in your area and what it is particularly good or bad for growing.
- how much of the land in your area is used for farming, etc. and how much is used for buildings and industry.
- if/how the land use in your area has changed in the last twenty-five years.

Garden vocabulary

How many of these words for different kinds of flowers, herbs, vegetables and fruit can you name in your own language?

1. Look the words up in your dictionary.
2. Group the words under the headings Flowers, Herbs, Vegetables and Fruit.
3. Make a wordsearch or crossword for your partner using at least ten of the words.

anemone	forget-me-not	parsley
asparagus	geranium	pea
basil	grape	pink
beans	hollyhock	poppy
bluebells	honeysuckle	primrose
busy lizzie	hyacinth	radish
buttercups	iris	rose
carnation	ivy	rosemary
carrot	jasmin	runner bean
catnip	lavender	spinach
cauliflower	lemon balm	snowdrop
cherry	lettuce	sunflower
chives	lilac	tarragon
cress	lobelia	thistle
crocus	marigold	thyme
daffodil	mint	tomato
daisy	onions	tulip
dill	orange	turnip
fern	pansie	violet

7.4

Easter

Easter in America

Easter has only been celebrated on a widescale in the USA since the end of the Civil War (1861-1865). Although it is mainly a Christian festival it is also celebrated by non-Christians and many pagan symbols and customs are associated with it. Indeed, the name Easter itself is probably not of Christian origin but more likely comes from the name of the Anglo-Saxon goddess of Spring, Eostre. Chocolate Easter eggs or hard-boiled eggs dyed in bright colours as well as the Easter bunny are typically associated with Easter in America, and these too derive from pagan times and are signs of fertility. Other typical symbols of Easter – all of which are often seen on Easter cards – are baby chicks or ducks, pussy willow and Easter lilies. Easter lilies are traditionally used to decorate churches at Easter. Children in America enjoy special egg hunts on Easter Sunday: they have to find baskets full of sweets and candy which have been hidden in the house or yard. They also take part in Easter egg rolls: they have to roll as many boiled eggs as possible down a slope without breaking the shells.
On Easter Monday the famous White House Egg Roll takes place on the lawn of the White House in Washington D. C. and many families go there to watch and take part.
Easter Sunday is traditionally a family day for most Americans. Relatives and friends go to church in the morning and then have dinner together. They often eat ham or, if the weather is good enough, go on picnics. On Easter Sunday people also often dress up in special spring clothes for the first time after the winter.

When is Easter?

The date of Easter is different each year. Easter Sunday is the first Sunday after the first full moon after the spring equinox! It can be any time between 22nd March and 25th April.
Follow the instructions below and you can work out the date of Easter in a given year.
To work out the date of Easter in a particular year you need to know the Golden number and the Sunday letter which goes with that year. When you have worked out the Golden number and the Sunday letter you can find the date on the table below. Here's how to find the date of Easter in the year 2000.

1. To find the Golden number of the year 2000:
a) Add 1 to the year: 2000 + 1 = 2001
b) Divide the number you get by 19: 2001/19 = 105 remainder 3
The Golden number is the remainder: 3.

2. To find the Sunday letter for the year 2000:
a) Divide the year by 4: 2000/4 = 500 (If there is a remainder when you divide by 4, just ignore it!)
b) Add together the number of the year and the number you got in part 2a): 2000 + 500 = 2500
c) Add 6 to the number you get: 2500 + 6 = 2506
d) Divide the result by 7: 2506/7 = 358 remainder 0.

The Sunday letter for each year depends on the remainder:

Remainder: 0 = Sunday letter: A
Remainder: 1 = Sunday letter: G
Remainder: 2 = Sunday letter: F
Remainder: 3 = Sunday letter: E
Remainder: 4 = Sunday letter: D
Remainder: 5 = Sunday letter: C
Remainder: 6 = Sunday letter: B

The year 2000 has the Golden number 3 and the Sunday letter A.
So Easter Sunday in the year 2000 is on March 26th.

Now work out the date of Easter Sunday
a) next year
b) in five years' time
c) in 10 years' time.

Golden Number	A	B	C	D	E	F	G
1	April 16	17	18	19	20	21	15
2	April 9	10	4	5	6	7	8
3	Mar. 26	27	28	29	30	24	25
4	April 16	17	18	12	13	14	15
5	April 2	3	4	5	6	7	1
6	April 23	24	25	19	20	21	22
7	April 9	10	11	12	13	14	15
8	April 2	3	4	Mar. 29	30	31	April 1
9	April 23	17	18	19	20	21	22
10	April 9	10	11	12	6	7	8
11	Mar. 26	27	28	29	30	31	April 1
12	April 16	17	18	19	20	14	15
13	April 9	3	4	5	6	7	8
14	Mar. 26	27	28	29	23	24	25
15	April 16	17	11	12	13	14	15
16	April 2	3	4	5	6	Mar. 31	April 1
17	April 23	24	18	19	20	21	22
18	April 9	10	11	12	13	14	8
19	April 2	3	Mar. 28	29	30	31	April 1

Egg Trouble Again
by Norman Hunter

A great calm settled over the royal palace of Incrediblania. The Queen had given up rushing round tidying the ornaments. The King refrained from sticking his little finger out when drinking tea. The Prime Minister stopped washing behind his ears every day and the royal cat came out from under the bed.
For, oh joyous and relaxing news, the Grand Congress of the Twenty Nations was over. The kings and Oriental monarchs had all gone home.
'Thank goodness for that,' exclaimed the Queen, kicking her shoes off and putting her feet up, something she hadn't dared to do while the visiting monarchs were all over the place. 'No more royal banquets. No more wearing of best clothes every day. No more frightful entertainments to keep the monarchs happy. And we can put the best tablecloths away and use the old drip-dry, non-iron ones which save a lot of work.'
'Well, at least the Congress did one good thing,' said the King, carefully putting away the real imperial crown that was solid gold and very heavy and getting out his every-day plastic one that was nice and light but not magnificent enough for wearing when they had visitors. 'At least it taught you how to boil eggs.'
'Yes, it did,' agreed the Queen, 'but now the Congress is over and we're by ourselves again I needn't do it any more. Cook is quite capable of boiling eggs for breakfast, I'm sure.'
But next morning's breakfast was not a success. 'My egg's all runny,' complained the King, 'and you know I like it hard-boiled. I'm tired of soft, runny eggs after all that practising you did before the Congress, giving me eggs boiled three minutes only.'
'It's all right for you to complain,' said the Queen.
'I've got a hard-boiled egg and you know I like mine soft so that I can dip fingers of bread and butter in it. I can't think how it's happened.'
'Well,' said the King, 'we never had boiled eggs for breakfast before the Congress and so perhaps the palace kitchen isn't really geared up to boiling eggs. Anyway, let's just change them round,' he whispered. 'There aren't any foreign monarchs here to see us do it.'
'Tut, tut!' whispered the Queen. 'How can you suggest such a thing? There may not be any royal monarchs here but we've still got the Butler and the footmen looking on. If we go changing eggs at breakfast it'll be all over the kingdom in no time. "Egg changing at the palace," the newspapers will scream. "Soft-boiled eggs make it hard for the King."
'Fetch the Cook!' said the King to the Butler.
The Cook said she was sorry about the eggs and it wouldn't happen again.
But it did. Next morning the King's egg was soft again and the Queen's was hard.
And the same thing happened again the next morning.
'Fetch the Cook!' cried the Queen, banging the marmalade pot on the table.
'Now, listen to me, Gertrude,' cried the Queen. 'You say you put the King's egg on the left side of the tray and mine on the right. But my egg was hard again this morning and the King's was soft. It won't do, you know. What is the matter in the kitchen? Is your egg-timer slow, or haven't you got a cookery book?'
'P-p-please, Your Majesty,' stuttered the Cook, wiping a floury hand nervously all over her face, 'I do try to boil Your Majesty's eggs soft, really I do! I boil them less and less each day.'
The cook put the King's next egg on to boil at lunch-time.

And the next day she didn't even boil the Queen's egg at all. She just sponged its face with warm water. But, would you believe it, the Queen's egg was as hard as a stone bullet and the King's was so runny he could hardly catch it with his spoon.

'Really, this is too bad!' cried the King. 'Any plumber or bus driver in the kingdom can have his eggs hard-boiled, yet I, His Imperial Majesty the King of Incrediblania, have to put up with them runny. It's awful, it's frightful, it's treason!'

'Disgraceful!' roared the Queen. 'Tomorrow morning I shall be graciously pleased to jolly well cook the eggs myself.'

Next morning the Cook and the kitchen maids all put on their best clothes and the Queen came in with a special little egg-boiling saucepan with the royal arms on it.

'Now, I will show you how our eggs should be cooked,' said Her Majesty. And, taking an egg from a velvet cushion held by a footman, she dropped it into the saucepan.

She counted up to a hundred, sang the choruses of all the songs she knew, and finally she said, 'That should be done by now.'

With a gold spoon she took the hard-boiled egg out of the saucepan and put it in an egg-cup on the left side of the breakfast tray.

'That's the King's,' she said. 'Now for mine.'

And, taking another egg from the velvet cushion she popped it into the saucepan of already boiling water, and said, 'Two, four, six, eight, ten,' so quickly that nobody had time to join in. Then she took the egg out again, putting it into an egg-cup on the right side of the tray.

'Now bring them in,' she commanded, 'and we shall see.'

The King broke his egg very neatly without getting any shell in it.

The Queen broke hers not quite so neatly.
'Hard-boiled!' she shrieked.
'Runnier than ever!' yelled the King.
'Impossible!!' cried the Queen. 'It can't have happened, and yet it has! I put your hard-boiled egg on the left side of the tray.'
'Well, I took the one on the left side of the tray,' said the King. 'And it was runny, so there!'

At that moment the Lord Chamberlain came into the room.

'Excuse me,' he said. 'I know a lot about eggs, because I was born on Easter Monday. I know why Your Majesties' eggs always go wrong. Call the Cook,' he cried, 'and tell her to boil one egg hard and one soft, mark them with a pencil and bring them to me.'

'All right,' said the Cook when she was told, although she had made up her mind to leave next day, eggs or no eggs.

She brought them in.

'Now,' said the Lord Chamberlain, 'I place the egg marked "hard" on the left of the tray for the King. The egg marked "soft" I place here, on the right, for Her Majesty the Queen.'

'Yes,' said the King, the Queen and the Cook.
'Well,' said the King, the Queen and the Cook.
'Well,' said the Lord Chamberlain, 'when the Butler picks up the tray the hard egg is on his left and the soft one on his right. But when he hands the tray to Your Majesties, you take the eggs from the opposite side of the tray and so you each get the wrong one.'
'Well, of course!' cried the Queen. 'The hard egg is on our right, and the soft one is on our left. Oh dear, why don't we always mark the eggs "hard" and "soft" in future, and then we'll be sure to get the right ones?'

The King didn't answer. He was busy enjoying his first hard-boiled egg for ages and wasn't going to be put off by anything.

APRIL FOOLS' DAY

April Fools' Day – spelling test
Circle all the mistakes in the following text about April Fools' Day. Then try to find the correct spelling for the "fool" words.

> **Good News**
> The Board of Education has just set up new rules. That in the future they'll shut all the schools. On every April Fools'.
> APRIL FOOL!
> (Keep cool.)
>
> William Cole

About April Fouls' Day

April Fouls' Day is on April 1st. People all over the world play tricks on each uther on this day! No-one quite nows when April Fouls' Day was first cellebrated. There are different theorys. But it propaply dates back to ancient times when the Spring equinnox marked the begining of the New Year. April 1st may well have bean the last day of a weak of New Year festivities.

The idea of playing tricks on April 1st propaply begann in France in 1564. It was then that the Franch desided to change their calender. January 1st became New Year's Day. It had previously bean the custom to exchange New Year presents and messages on April 1st, and so now joke presents and messages were given on April 1st in memary of the old New Year's Day! Maybe some people even forgott that the dates had bean changed and still cellebrated New Year's weak at the end of March. These people might have bean the first April fouls!

The April foul custem spread from France throughought Europa and to America. On one April Foul's Day in Britian in the 19th century lots of people gathered at the Tower of London because they had received invitations to wash 'the anual cerremony of watching the white lions'. This was, of course, a joke, which many people fell for! Nowadays spoof reports are published in many newspapers and broadcast on television, often making April Fouls of thowsands of people! One famos TV programe on April 1st reported on the spagetti harvest in Italy. It showed workers pricking spagetti from trees! Children and young people especially enjoy playing tricks. One tipical trick, which is very easy and effective, is simply to stand somewhere public and lock up or point at the sky as if you have scene something. You then just wait for other people to join in. There is however one wrule about playing tricks on April Fouls' Day in Britain: all jokes must be played by noon. If you play a trick on someone after twelve o'clock you are the April Fool!

How many mistakes did you find?

Score:

More than 45: You are excellent at marking. If you become a school teacher children will not like you!

38–45: Not bad!

30–37: Quite poor! If you become a school teacher children will love you!

Less than 30: Perhaps you need glasses!

Mother's Day

Mother's Day, or Mothering Sunday, as it is called in Britain, is celebrated on a different date in Britain and America.

Mothering Sunday in Britain is always the fourth Sunday in Lent. It is also called Mid-Lent Sunday and has been celebrated for more than three hundred years. It dates back to the 17th century when the fourth Sunday in Lent was the one day in the middle of the period of fasting when games and feasting were allowed.

Apprentices and servants working away from home were given the day off to visit their families. On their way home they would pick flowers, especially primroses and violets, to give to their mothers. This custom became known as going "a-mothering". A simnel cake, a rich fruit cake, was another traditional gift given to mothers.

Nowadays, flowers and chocolates are typical presents and Mother's Day cards are sent to mothers and grandmothers. What started as a religious celebration has changed now to a rather commercialized event.

In America, Mother's Day is celebrated on the second Sunday in May. On this day Americans put up the flag to draw special attention to all the mothers and grandmothers of their country. People give cards and presents and often bouquets of carnations.

Mother's Day has been celebrated in America since 1914. In May 1907, a woman called Miss Anna M. Jarvis, persuaded her church in Grafton, West Virginia, to hold a church service in honour of her mother who had died two years before. Anna M. Jarvis gave money for the church and she bought five hundred carnations – her mother's favourite flower – to give out to all the mothers in the church. Anna's mother, Mrs Reeves Jarvis, had been the mother of eleven children, but seven of them died when they were still young. Mrs Reeves Jarvis had been a "mother" to the communities in which she had lived. She had been a Sunday school teacher and she had organized a "Mother's Friendship Day" to help people from both sides of the American Civil War to become friends. The people of Grafton were very proud of her.

In 1908, the anniversary of Mrs Reeves Jarvis' death was officially celebrated as "Mother's Day" by the church in Grafton. Everyone wore a carnation during the service. In that year, Anna Jarvis started a campaign to have a special day declared in honour of all mothers. She wrote letters to congressmen and other important people. In 1910, the first state "Mother's Day" was celebrated in West Virginia. Soon, several states followed. People were asked to go to church on that day, and carnations continued to be associated with the day.

On May 8, 1914, President Woodrow Wilson made the first Mother's Day Proclamation. Mother's Day became part of American law, and the second Sunday in May was set aside for this special occasion.

Statement	True for Mothering Sunday in Britain	True for Mother's Day in the USA
1. It is a day when love and respect is shown for mothers and grandmothers.		
2. It dates back to the 17th century.		
3. It was first celebrated in May 1908.		
4. It is always celebrated on the second Sunday in May.		
5. It is always celebrated on the fourth Sunday in Lent.		
6. Carnations are traditionally associated with this day.		
7. Simnel cakes used to be a traditional gift for mothers on this day.		
8. Anna M. Jarvis started a campaign to have a special day declared in honour of all mothers.		
9. It used to be the only day in Lent when games could be played.		
10. People working away from home were given the day off to visit their families.		
11. West Virginia was the first state to adopt an official Mother's Day.		
12. Today it has become a rather commericalized event.		

A Change in the Earth's Climate

The ozone hole, the greenhouse effect, acid rain – just three of many of the problems which the environment of the Earth is facing. What exactly are these problems? And what effect are they having on our climate and our environment?

The greenhouse effect is the term used to describe the way pollution has affected the atmosphere and the way the sun's energy is heating the Earth up as a result. Over the past few hundred years – and especially in the last century – people have been using more and more fuel (wood, coal, oil, gas and petrol) to heat their homes, run their machines and drive their vehicles. When these fuels burn, gases such as carbon dioxide (CO_2) are formed. These gases are now building up in the atmosphere. The problem is made worse by the fact that the tropical rain forests are getting smaller and smaller and so there are less trees which can absorb carbon dioxide during the day. The increase of carbon dioxide in the air has made it easier for the atmosphere to take in the sun's heat, but like in a greenhouse, the heat and light can get in but not out again. As a result the Earth's atmosphere may heat up. This is known as global warming. If the Earth becomes warmer, the ice caps may melt causing flooding and the Earth's weather patterns may change. These changes in the climate would affect farming and vegetation and could lead to hunger and disease.

Acid rain is caused by the gases which are released from power stations, factory chimneys and vehicle exhausts. The most dangerous of these gases are sulphur and nitrogen oxides (SO_2 and Ox). These gases react with other gases in the atmosphere to create mild sulphuric and nitric acids (H_2SO_4 and HNO_3). The acids combine with the water in the atmosphere in clouds and then fall back to earth as so-called acid rain. Depending on the weather and wind at the time, acid rain clouds can travel hundreds of miles. The acid rain can then fall far away from the factories which caused it. Acid rain destroys trees, poisons soil, damages plants and crops, pollutes the water in lakes and rivers killing fish and other waterlife, and eats away stonework and metalwork on buildings. It is also thought to affect human health by causing increased bronchitis, for example.

To understand what the ozone 'hole' is, we first need to know what ozone and the ozone layer are. Ozone is a three atom molecule of oxygen, which is capable of absorbing ultra-violet light. Although ozone only makes up a very small part (less than one part per million) of all the gases in the atmosphere, it alone absorbs most of the sun's dangerous ultra-violet light. The ozone layer is between 12 to 24 kilometres above the Earth. It is a layer in the upper atmosphere with a high concentration of ozone. The ozone layer acts as a kind of shield, stopping the sun's dangerous ultra-violet rays getting to the Earth. In recent years particular gases, called chlorofluorocarbons, which are commonly used in aerosol sprays and refrigerators, have been released into the atmosphere. These gases cause a series of complex reactions, the result of which is to rob the ozone molecules of their third atom, so that they become the same as normal atmospheric oxygen. Of course this normal oxygen cannot absorb ultra-violet light. As more and more ozone molecules are destroyed, the ozone layer gets thinner and thinner and could even disappear completely. This is known as the ozone 'hole'. The less ozone in the upper atmosphere, the larger the ozone hole. The larger the ozone hole, the larger the amounts of ultra-violet light which can reach the Earth. An increase in ultra-violet light is known to cause skin cancers and to damage crops and sea-life.

London Trip

When we went up to London
The coach was blue and white.
We went all round the Tower
And we saw just every sight.
We visited the V & A,
We visited the zoo,
And went and watched the Palace Guards
And saw things soldiers do.

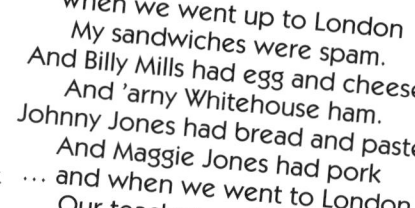

When we went up to London
My sandwiches were spam.
And Billy Mills had egg and cheese
And 'arny Whitehouse ham.
Johnny Jones had bread and paste
And Maggie Jones had pork
… and when we went to London
Our teacher made us walk!

COME ON, IT'S JUST AROUND THE NEXT CORNER!

CAN'T WE TAKE THE BUS?

We walked all round Trafalgar Square,
We walked all round St. Paul's
And whispered things that didn't work
On whispering gallery walls.

When we went up to London
The top came off my drink
And ran all down my trousers –
And made a nasty stink …
It got all on the coach seats,
It trickled on the floor,
It trickled on Miss Gardner's bag,
It trickled through the door …

The Science Museum was not too bad –
The toilets there were fun,
We played a game called pull the chain
– and slam the doors – and run.
We chased around the old steam trains,
We pulled those pulley things –
And Martin Knight – he pulled one off
And snapped those bits with springs.

The Albert Hall was really bad,
The Tate was boring too …
And that was when poor Enid White
Spilt all her curried stew.
… The man in there got really cross
He shouted REALLY LOUD
And everyone came running round and
Formed a great big crowd.

SLAM

Miss Gardner … well …
She sees this crowd,
And smells the curried stew,
And guesses that it's Enid White,
The way that teachers do –
And so – you see – we had to go
(though we'd wiped the pictures clean),
But the journey on the bus back home
Was the best that's ever been!
Norman had a pigeon
He'd got in Trafalgar Square
And he said it had a broken wing,
'til it flew up in the air!
It flew all round the driver's cab
It landed in his hair!
And made him wind the window down,
And curse, and yell, and swear.

Miss Gardner – she got really cross,
And made poor Norman cry,
He really thought the bird was hurt
and couldn't hardly fly.
And then we got the punctures.
We got three in a row,
And stuck in Blackwall Tunnel,
When the engine wouldn't go.
We had four smashing breakdowns,
The driver lost his way
We were five hours late returning
From a really super day!

Three cheers for Miss Gardner and our driver,
Hip … Hip …!!!

(Peter Dixon)

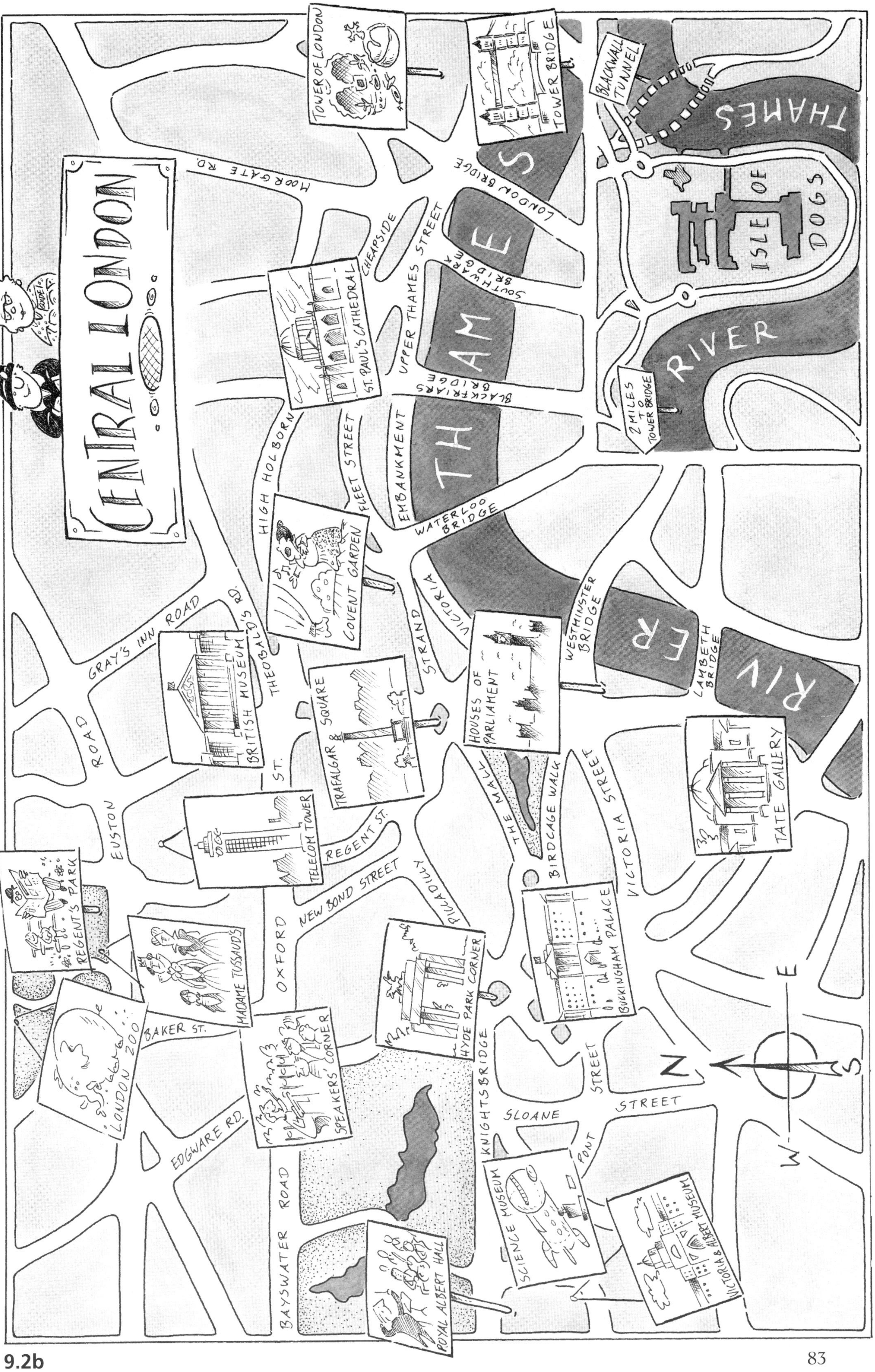

CENTRAL LONDON
TOWER OF LONDON
TOWER BRIDGE
BLACKWALL TUNNEL
THAMES
ISLE OF DOGS
RIVER
2 MILES TO TOWER BRIDGE
MOORGATE RD.
LONDON BRIDGE
CHEAPSIDE
UPPER THAMES STREET
SOUTHWARK BRIDGE
ST. PAUL'S CATHEDRAL
BLACKFRIARS BRIDGE
THAMES
HIGH HOLBORN
FLEET STREET
EMBANKMENT
WATERLOO BRIDGE
COVENT GARDEN
VICTORIA
STRAND
WESTMINSTER BRIDGE
RIVER
LAMBETH BRIDGE
GRAY'S INN ROAD
THEOBALD'S RD.
BRITISH MUSEUM
TRAFALGAR SQUARE
HOUSES OF PARLIAMENT
THE MALL
BIRDCAGE WALK
VICTORIA STREET
TATE GALLERY
EUSTON ROAD
ST.
TELECOM TOWER
REGENT ST.
NEW BOND STREET
PICCADILLY
OXFORD
REGENT'S PARK
MADAME TUSSAUDS
BUCKINGHAM PALACE
HYDE PARK CORNER
BAKER ST.
SPEAKERS' CORNER
KNIGHTSBRIDGE
LONDON ZOO
EDGWARE RD.
SLOANE STREET
PONT STREET
N
E
S
W
BAYSWATER ROAD
SCIENCE MUSEUM
ROYAL ALBERT HALL
VICTORIA & ALBERT MUSEUM

All American: Fourth of July and Flag Day

Fill in the gaps in the following text with words from the box below.

added – barbecues – blue – buildings – colonies – country – history – important – independence – Independence Day – open – parades – put out – red – stars – states – states – stripes – signed – white

Only five national bank holidays in the USA today are celebrated in all of the states. These are Labor Day (the first Monday in September), Thanksgiving Day (the fourth Thursday in November), Christmas Day, New Year's Day and _____ (the 4th July). Independence Day is one of the most _____ holidays in the USA. It commemorates the day when the United States declared its _____ from Britain – on 4th July, 1776. The Declaration of Independence was _____ in Independence Hall, Pennsylvania, and this document marks the beginning of the _____ of the United States of America. On 4th July flags and decorations are _____ in the streets and on public buildings. Every village, town and city has _____, games or rodeos. Some people have picnics and _____, others go on trips to the beach or to the _____, and in the evening there are magnificent firework displays to celebrate America's birthday.

Flag Day is celebrated on 14th June. It commemorates the day in 1777 when the Stars and Stripes became the official flag of the USA. The flag has thirteen alternate _____ of _____ and _____, which represent the thirteen _____ that became independent from Britain in 1776. The white stars on the _____ background indicate the number of _____ in the union. As each new state was adopted, another star was _____ to the original thirteen, and there are now 50 altogether. The last two _____ to join the Union were Alaska, in 1959 and Hawaii, in 1960. On Flag Day the Stars and Stripes is displayed in front of most public and many private _____. Flag Day is not a public holiday in the USA, so banks, schools, offices and businesses stay _____.

American flag in 1776

American flag today

American English (AE) – British English (BE)

1. Match these American English (AE) words to their British English (BE) equivalents.
   Look up any of the words you do not know in a dictionary.
   You can look up both the British or the American words.
2. Learn the words together with your partner(s). Read the words aloud two or three times.
   Ask your partner questions, such as: "What is 'cinema' in American English?" or
   "What is 'fall' in British English?"
   Your partner must answer the questions and then ask the next question.
3. When you know the meanings of all the words on the sheet, play the game.
   One, two or three players can play.

| AE: apartment | = | BE: flat | | AE: backpack | = | BE: rucksack |

AE ✂ BE

AE: apartment	AE: parking lot	BE: autumn	BE: lift
AE: backpack	AE: railroad	BE: biscuit	BE: lorry
AE: bill	AE: rest-room	BE: bonnet	BE: nappy
AE: cookie	AE: sidewalk	BE: boot	BE: note
AE: diaper	AE: subway	BE: caravan	BE: pavement
AE: elevator	AE: trailer	BE: car park	BE: petrol
AE: fall	AE: trunk	BE: cinema	BE: railway
AE: first floor	AE: truck	BE: crossroads	BE: rucksack
AE: gas	AE: undershirt	BE: dummy	BE: toilet
AE: hood	AE: vacation	BE: flat	BE: toilet bag
AE: intersection	AE: washbag	BE: give way sign	BE: underground
AE: movies	AE: yield sign	BE: ground floor	BE: vest
AE: pacifier		BE: holiday(s)	

A pairs game

The aim of the game is to find pairs of words which have the same meaning but are different in American English and British English.

1. Cut out all the words along the lines to make cards.
2. Put the cards on the table – face down.
3. The first player turns over two cards. If they make a pair the player can keep them and turn over two more cards. If they are not a pair the cards must be turned over again.
4. The player with most cards at the end is the winner.

9.4

Last day – at last!

Last Day of the Summer Term

We sit around in the classroom
Exchanging holiday plans;
The many familiar faces –
Kate's and Maud's and Anne's!

Kate's spending a month in Brighton;
Joan is for Paris; Maud's
Going to an aunt in Scotland,
And Anne to the Norfolk Broads.

I listen, envious and silent,
Or do the jobs of the day;
Tidy up; stack books; or I read
In a half-hearted sort of way.

We gather for the last Assembly –
The prayers and the final hymn:
'If you girls go on being fidgety
I shall keep the whole school in.'

But it's over at last, all over;
And I walk along home with Sue,
And stand at her door, while she chatters
About what they're going to do:

They've hired a holiday-caravan
Down on the Isle of Wight:
We shall set out by car this evening –
We'll be travelling all night …

'Ah, well! Good-bye till September!'
I go on to my house alone;
I find my key, and enter
My holiday-home.

The house is close and quiet;
A few dead roses spill
Their petals one by one
On the hot window-sill.

A tap drips in the kitchen;
Two flies buzz on the pane;
There's a note on the breakfast-table:
Two lines from Mother. – 'Dear Jane,

'Make yourself a cup of tea, dear;
I'll be working late at the shop.'
And I turn with hardly a sigh
To the uncleared washing-up;

Or wander vaguely upstairs,
To stare awhile at the tall
Unanswering photo of father
That hangs on my bedroom wall.

(John Walsh)

Bad Report – Good Manners

My daddy said, 'My son, my son,
This school report is bad.'
I said, 'I did my best I did,
My dad my dad my dad.'
'Explain, my son, my son,' he said,
'Why bottom of the class?'
'I stood aside, my dad my dad,
To let the others pass.'

(Spike Milligan)

SUBJECT REPORT

SUBJECT ~~French~~/German	NAME Laura Donner	GUILD Fisher	~~CLASS~~/SET 9B

CONTENT/SKILLS	Achievement Level ✱							COMMENTS
	1	2	3	4	5	6	7	
Speaking		✓						
Reading Comprehension		✓						
Written Exercises			✓					
Listening Comprehension			✓					

Comments:
School exam
Writing : 15½/25
Reading : 25/30
Listening : 17½/30
Speaking : 14/20

Laura's German has improved noticeably since she took part in the school exchange.

EFFORT/ATTITUDE								
Interested, works and participates well							✓	
Usually works well								
Needs to concentrate, greater application needed								
A significant change of attitude required								

SUBJECT TEACHER G Brown   Date July 1996

1. The Scale 1 to 7 refers to the individual's performance in each of the content/skills listed for the subject.
2. Grade 1 is the highest and Grade 7 the lowest.
3. Where the grading relates to class or set rather than across the year this is indicated✱.

****European countries and their capital cities****

How many of these European countries and their capital cities do you know? Write down the names on a separate piece of paper.

Make a wordsearch puzzle for your partner.
1. Write a list of six European countries and their capital cities on a separate sheet of paper.
2. Hide your words in the grid below (across or down). Use all capital letters.
3. Give your partner your puzzle and take your partner's puzzle.
4. Set a time limit for finding the words, e.g. five minutes.
5. Both start at the same time.
6. Circle the words in the puzzle and write them on the list on the worksheet.
7. Compare your words with your partner's original list. Tick them off on both lists.
8. You get a point for each word you have found in your partner's puzzle and written on the list. Your partner gets a point for each word he or she has found in your puzzle.
9. The winner is the player who has found the most words.

Country	Capital City
1 _____	_____
2 _____	_____
3 _____	_____
4 _____	_____
5 _____	_____
6 _____	_____

10.2

87

The Round Europe Race

(Place question cards here)